How to Find a Ghost

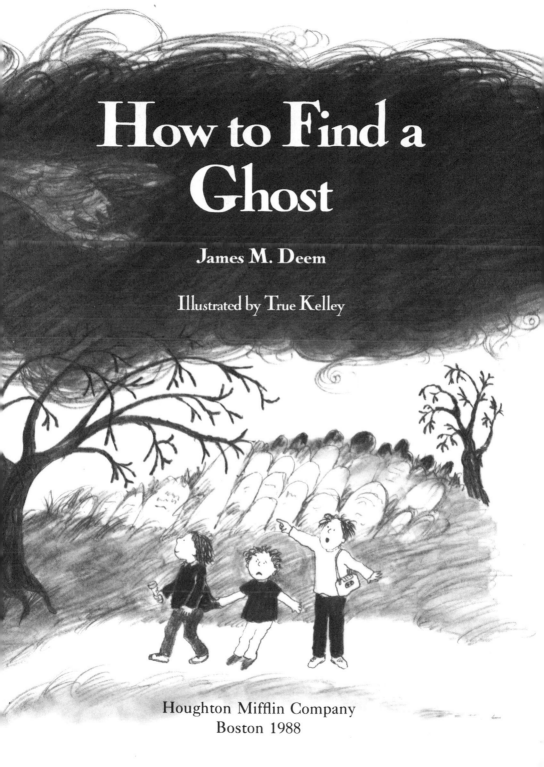

How to Find a Ghost

James M. Deem

Illustrated by True Kelley

Houghton Mifflin Company
Boston 1988

For Anna and Rachel,
twin ghosthunters

Library of Congress Cataloging-in-Publication Data

Deem, James M.
  How to find a ghost.

  Bibliography: p.
  Includes index.
  Summary: Discusses the characteristics of ghosts
with descriptions of sightings and instructions for
becoming a ghost detective.
    1. Ghosts—Juvenile literature.   2. Psychical
research—Juvenile literature.   [1. Ghosts.
2. Supernatural.   3. Psychical research]   I. Kelley,
True, ill.   II. Title.
BF1461.D44   1988   133.1   88-649
ISBN 0-395-46846-9

Printed in the United States of America

A 10 9 8 7 6 5 4 3 2 1

Contents

Introduction

"Why can't I see a ghost?"

If you've ever asked that question, you're not alone. At one time or another, almost everyone wants to see a ghost. Maybe you can't see a ghost because you don't know what one looks like. Maybe you can't find one because you don't know where to search. Most of all, maybe you don't really understand what ghosts are and why they haunt people and places.

Of course, the other possibility is that if you don't know what ghosts look like, you may have seen one already. Maybe that person you saw one day who seemed a little odd was a ghost. Maybe that shadow you saw in your bedroom one night was one. Perhaps the knocking you've heard in the basement or on your window was caused by a ghost.

Instead of asking *why* you can't see a ghost, perhaps the question you should be asking is, "*How* can I see a ghost?"

If you're sure you want to know the answer, keep reading. The first part of this book describes what ghosts look like, where they come from, where you can find them, and what you might do if you're sure you *want* to find one. If you happen to meet any ghosts, the book also gives you advice on what to do next, so that you can prove your ghost was real. By the time you finish the book, you should be an expert ghosthunter.

Throughout the book, real ghost stories, mostly from the United States and England, serve as examples. These stories aren't tall tales and legends that were invented in some writers' imaginations. In fact, most were reported by ordinary people, and many were even studied by scientists. Some are spooky, and some aren't. But all of them are real.

Whenever possible, I have tried to give the exact location of the haunting and to use the observers' real names. Many times, though, people want to preserve their privacy, and I have respected that by providing pseudonyms when necessary. If a location was not identified, however, I did not invent one. When I have used dialogue, it was either contained in or strongly suggested by the original accounts. Finally, in only a few cases did I find it necessary to simplify some rather complex hauntings.

If you do come across any ghosts or see any strange happenings after reading this book, write me at the following address: James M. Deem, % Houghton Mifflin, Two Park Street, Boston, Massachusetts 02108. Describe your ghost or your experience completely. Maybe next time I'll be able to refer to your ghost story.

Above all, happy ghost hunting!

1. Testing Your Ghost IQ

Do you know the real facts about ghosts? Before you can find a ghost, you need to know the truth about them. Ask yourself the following questions to see what kind of ghost facts you already know.

The Ghost IQ Test

1. Are ghosts usually white and misty-looking?
2. If a person dies a violent death and becomes a ghost, will the ghost be disfigured?
3. Do most ghosts walk through furniture?
4. Is it true that you can't see a ghost's reflection in a mirror?
5. Do most ghosts like to frighten people?
6. Is it true that ghosts can't talk?
7. Do ghosts enjoy playing tricks on people?
8. Can you see through a ghost?
9. Do all ghosts look as though they're dead?
10. Do people become ghosts because they died tragic deaths?
11. Is it true that ghosts never repeat the same activity twice?
12. Do most ghosts do interesting things?
13. Is it true that two people can't see the same ghost at the same time?
14. Can ghosts be seen only after sundown and before sunrise?
15. Do ghosts look like strange, frightening creatures?

Now, turn the page and see what kind of ghost expert you are.

The Ghost IQ Test Answers:
You may be surprised to learn
that all of the answers to the test are "no."

Most people have a number of wrong ideas about ghosts. Yes, ghosts can appear and disappear suddenly. They can also pass through solid walls and closed doors. Sometimes they may appear to glide slightly above the floor. Otherwise, ghosts are very different from our common conception of them. Here are three of the most common mistaken ideas about ghosts:

Mistaken Idea 1: *Where ghosts come from*

Most people think that ghosts are dead people who haunt the living. They think that ghosts come about when people die horrible, tragic deaths. If a young woman dies in a car accident on her wedding night, for example, she will return to haunt her husband. Or if an

6

old man is murdered by an escaped convict, the ghost of the old man will haunt the convict and drive him crazy. While there may be some truth to these ideas, they don't tell the whole story about ghosts.

First, ghosts are not always the spirits of dead people. Sometimes people see the ghost of a person who is still living. A woman may see a friend of hers walking down the road, even though she finds out later that her friend was in another town, many miles away. Maybe she was thinking about her friend and somehow made her figure appear on the road. What's more, some people have reported seeing themselves as ghosts, even though they are still alive and healthy. A young boy may see a ghost that looks like him, walking out of his bedroom closet. No one knows why this happens, but it does on occasion.

Second, most people, even those who die tragic

deaths, don't become ghosts when they die; if they did, there would probably be more ghosts than people. You see, no one knows why people become ghosts. One popular idea is that ghosts may be people who become trapped in time. Perhaps a woman who loved walking through her garden when she was alive will repeat that walk over and over again as a ghost; she might have walked that path so many times that her memory will always haunt the garden. Or a man who, on his death-bed, asked for a certain wish may become a ghost to make sure that his wish is carried out. Even more puzzling is the fact that some ghosts haunt a place for many years, while other ghosts are seen only once and vanish forever. No one knows why this happens.

Finally, ghosts don't even have to be people. Did you know that as many as 20 percent of all ghost sightings reported, according to one survey, are ghosts of animals or objects? The most common animal ghosts are dogs and cats, which is understandable, since they are the most popular pets. There is no common type of object

ghost, however. People have reported ghost letters, ghost coats, ghost cars, and even ghost towns. One moment the object will be visible; then it is gone and the observer discovers that it could not have been there.

It's not surprising that scientists can't decide whether ghosts are real or not. Some say they are hallucinations (that is, something people only imagine that they see), while others say they are real. Other scientists are sure that seeing a ghost is like having a waking dream and reliving part of the past. But this doesn't explain the many times when ghosts are seen by two or more people at once could a group of people be having the same dream?

Since we know so little about ghosts, some scientists believe that the person who sees the ghost is more important than the ghost itself. They believe that some people who are more sensitive to supernatural experiences may have more ability to see ghosts than other, less sensitive people. Perhaps their minds are able to travel back in time to see a person who is now dead. But even if this is true, someone may live forty or fifty years before he sees a ghost. If that person had the ability to see ghosts, why didn't he see one sooner?

Some scientists also wonder if the country a person lives in affects his or her ability to see ghosts. A 1981 survey found that 42 percent of the people in Iceland had seen ghosts, while only 4 percent of the Chinese population of Hong Kong had. Before you take a plane to Iceland, however, the difference in the results might be explained by the fact that the Chinese people responding to the Hong Kong survey didn't trust the non-Chinese person doing the survey. Would you tell a stranger you didn't trust that you'd seen a ghost?

Even if some countries have more ghosts than others, why is that so? Does the weather or the climate affect the number of ghosts? Or is the personality of the ghost-hunter more important? The truth is that no one knows.

Mistaken Idea 2: *What ghosts look like*

What do you think ghosts look like? Do you picture them with white, misty bodies and large, dark eyes? Or do you think that ghosts look like zombies, with weird, disfigured faces?

The truth is that most ghosts aren't white and misty or disfigured. According to most people who have seen ghosts, they have the coloring and appearance of normal human beings, even if they died a violent death. They have solid bodies that can even be seen in a mirror.

Of course, there are always exceptions. Some people have seen ghosts who were white (or sometimes dark), filmy figures. Other people have seen ghosts whose bodies were solid on top but invisible on the bottom. Still others have seen ghosts who had wounds on their bodies or ghosts who looked dead rather than alive; the ghosts' faces may have been discolored, or their eyes may have been staring vacantly. But these kinds of ghosts are seen much less often than the "normal" kind.

Sometimes the only way to tell that a ghost is a ghost is by its clothing or by its complexion. If a person lived a long time ago, his ghost will probably be dressed in old-fashioned clothes. A ghost may also have a slightly — but noticeably — pale complexion.

So ghosts are usually not the strange, scary phantoms shown in the movies. In fact, you may have already seen a ghost and didn't know it, because it looked like a regular person.

I'M A GHOST!

NO! REALLY? ME TOO!

Mistaken Idea 3: *What ghosts do*

You might think that ghosts float down long, dark staircases in haunted houses, scream "Boo!" and then vanish into thin air — or, even worse, that they grab people who are foolish enough to walk through a cemetery after midnight and pull them into open graves.

Most people are surprised to find that ghosts do many of the same things that people do. Although ghosts may walk through walls as they disappear, they walk around furniture — not through it. They have also been reported to talk, although some scientists believe that ghosts use ESP rather than speech to communicate. In

11

this way, they think thoughts that are sent to the mind of the person they want to communicate with. This might sound like actual talking to the person, but it isn't. Finally, ghosts aren't active only at night in haunted houses or cemeteries; many prefer to be seen in broad daylight in very ordinary places.

Believe it or not, most ghosts lead pretty boring lives. Although ghosts in movies like *Poltergeist* or *Ghostbusters* or *The Amityville Horror* seem exciting, real ghosts are very different. They are more like the woman ghost I mentioned earlier who walks through her garden. What's more, they don't enjoy frightening anyone. The idea that ghosts jump out from behind tombstones or cellar doors or that they lurk about in the dark waiting to grab people is incorrect; ghosts just go about their business the way you go about yours. Of course, many people become so terrified when they see a ghost that they assume the ghost wanted to scare them, but this isn't so. In fact, a ghost may be just as frightened to see a person.

As you can see, ghosts are more complicated than you might have thought. They become even more complicated, though, when you discover, in the next two chapters, that there are at least six different kinds of ghosts.

2. Ghosts . . .

By now, you might be wondering how you'll recognize a ghost if you see one, especially if most ghosts look so normal. It's not as hard as you might think.

First, although the ghost may look like a real person, its face may be pale and its clothing may look old-fashioned.

Second, you may feel a chill. Many people who see a ghost report that they feel very cold right before they're aware of the ghost's presence. Persons who were in bed under a pile of blankets when they saw a ghost say that they were chilled to the bone before the ghost appeared. If you start to feel cold unexpectedly, either you're coming down with the flu — or you're about to have a haunting experience.

Third, if you're like most people, you'll be less than six feet away from the ghost and won't see it for very long. Ghosts usually appear for fifteen seconds or less. But get ready, just in case: some people report that they watched their ghosts for as long as five minutes.

Fourth, the ghost will probably disappear — or walk through a wall — in front of your eyes. If that happens, you'll know you've seen one.

Finally, even if you can't pinpoint the reason, you'll still know you've seen a ghost. According to one survey, more than two thirds of the people who've seen ghosts simply *know* they've seen one.

But there's more to ghost hunting than just realizing that you've seen one. It's important to know what kind you've seen. Did you know that just as there are different kinds of people, there are different kinds of ghosts? For this reason, it's hard to talk about ghosts as if they were all the same. Each one seems to have its own style and peculiar habits of haunting. Before you begin your own ghost hunt, you should know some of the different types of ghosts that you might find.

Ghost Type 1: *Ghosts of the dead who are seen repeatedly*

These are ghosts of people who lived many years ago and who are seen doing the same ghostly deeds over and over again. This kind of ghost rarely knows it is being watched; it simply performs its action, unaware of anything else. If the ghost does notice someone watching, it may look surprised and vanish.

An example of this kind of ghost has occurred in Pluckley, England, where the ghost of a Gypsy woman has been seen repeatedly. During the last part of her life, the woman picked watercress from nearby Pinnock Stream and then sold it to earn her meager living. After a tiring day of harvesting watercress, she liked to sit on a bridge, smoking her pipe and drinking. Unfortunately, the woman liked to drink a little too much. One night around sundown, she was careless as she drank: some of the alcohol from her gin bottle spilled onto her shawl. As she stopped to light her pipe, a spark shot onto her shawl. In a flash, it burst into flames, and she was quickly burned beyond recognition.

Ever since her death, the Gypsy's figure has been frequently seen by many different people, but always at the same time: sunset. She sits on the rail of the bridge, smoking her pipe. She never tries to communicate with anyone; her figure appears and then slowly dissolves in a reddish haze.

Seeing this kind of ghost is like listening to a record when the needle gets stuck. Just the way that the same section of the record is replayed, a small part of the Gypsy woman's life is repeated over and over again. Why this happens to some people and not others is unknown. Maybe the Gypsy loved sitting on the bridge so much that her memory lives on there. Or perhaps she appears at the bridge because she died so tragically there.

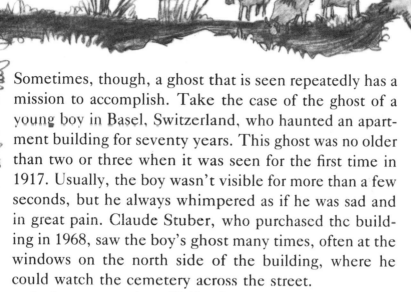

Sometimes, though, a ghost that is seen repeatedly has a mission to accomplish. Take the case of the ghost of a young boy in Basel, Switzerland, who haunted an apartment building for seventy years. This ghost was no older than two or three when it was seen for the first time in 1917. Usually, the boy wasn't visible for more than a few seconds, but he always whimpered as if he was sad and in great pain. Claude Stuber, who purchased the building in 1968, saw the boy's ghost many times, often at the windows on the north side of the building, where he could watch the cemetery across the street.

A ghost researcher, Haller Voisart, who heard about the haunting, suspected that the boy's body had never been buried. With Mr. Stuber's permission, Mr. Voisart searched the apartment building for clues to the haunting. On the second day, he discovered a dust-covered crib in the attic. In it, he found the boy's remains wrapped in a yellowed newspaper dated March 22, 1917. For seventy years, the boy's ghost had tried to communicate with the tenants of the building — to no avail. Finally, someone had helped him.

A few days later, the boy was buried in the cemetery. Since then, his ghost has not been seen.

Ghost Type 2: *Ghosts of the dead who are seen one or two times*

This type of ghost is similar to the first, except that it is seen only once or twice and then never appears again. Often, this ghost has a mission to accomplish.

For example, a young woman reported to ghosthunters Celia Green and Charles McCreery that her grandfather, before he died, was an important person in her life. Since he was a well-educated man, he took a special interest in her school work. He wanted to encourage her to attend college and choose a good career. For this reason, he liked to talk about the problems she was having in school. In turn, she felt that she could always confide in him because he understood her. When he died, around her eighteenth birthday, she was very upset.

Six months later, she had to face a serious problem in school — without her grandfather to help. But one night, about 3 A.M., she watched as her grandfather's ghost walked through her bedroom wall; his face was quite visible, well lit by a circle of gray light. The next morning, she discovered that she could resolve her problem. The ghost appeared once more a few months later when she needed help again. After that, it never returned.

Perhaps the grandfather, sensing his granddaughter's difficulty, returned to help her. He may have realized, though, that she needed to rely on herself to solve her problems. Interestingly enough, both times that she saw the ghost, the young woman was in her bedroom. Usually, a ghost that appears more than once is seen in the same place each time.

A much stranger case of a ghost seen only twice was reported by Dr. Karlis Osis, a ghost researcher at the American Society for Psychical Research. Leslie and Beth Smith had four children, but the youngest, whose name was Ricky, drowned when he was just eighteen months old. For over a year, Leslie and Beth and their parents tried to overcome their grief, but they missed Ricky terribly. Leslie, who had been especially fond of his young son, took up flying for a distraction.

One day in 1982, about a year and a half after Ricky's death, Leslie was on a business trip, flying his own plane across the southern part of the United States. After refueling for the second time and taking off for his final destination around 11:30 P.M., Leslie lost control of his plane and it crashed, killing him instantly.

Two nights later, Leslie's mother, Marge, grieving now for her son and her grandson, was awakened sometime after 1 A.M. by a disturbance in her room. She looked toward the foot of her bed and saw both Leslie and Ricky. Leslie was holding Ricky's hand, and they were looking at each other. As Marge told Dr. Osis, "They were content; they were happy that they found each other, that they were together now. And they were letting me know. . . ." Then their bodies faded away.

Marge's husband didn't wake up during the ghosts' visit, but there is good reason to believe that Marge did not imagine the experience. For, unknown to her, a few hours before Marge saw her son and grandson, they also paid a visit to Leslie's favorite niece, Jennifer, who was six years old at the time.

Jennifer was awake in her bedroom when she saw Leslie and Ricky holding hands. They stood in front of her, looking quite lifelike. Jennifer, too, experienced a feeling of peacefulness. When they disappeared, Jennifer immediately told her mother what she had seen.

This episode is quite unusual for a number of reasons. First, Marge and Jennifer did not tell each other what they had seen until days later. Yet they both had almost the same experience. Second, Leslie's and Ricky's ghosts appeared in two different places, 150 miles apart. Finally, Leslie and Ricky did not visit any other family members and were never seen again. It seems as if Leslie wanted to communicate his sense of happiness about his reunion with his son to his mother and his niece. Perhaps he chose to visit both in order to demonstrate that their experiences were real and not imagined. Perhaps he chose not to visit his wife, because his appearance might have served to upset her more.

Ghost Type 3: *Ghosts of the dying*

Some ghosts appear only at the time of a person's death. Many people have told of seeing a relative or a close friend, only to find out later that the person had died in another location around the time they saw him. This type of ghost wants to be seen by someone, as if to mark the time of death or to say goodbye.

Take the haunting of John Blaney, which was reported to the British Society for Psychical Research. On the morning of April 10, 1889, a young boy and his sister were walking down the stairs of their house when the boy spied a former servant standing in the kitchen.

"Why, there's John Blaney," he said, aware that Blaney's face seemed to be a sickly yellow color and that his eyes looked hollow. "I didn't know he was in the house!"

From her perch on the staircase, his sister looked into the kitchen but saw nothing. "No one's there. And anyway, John Blaney hasn't worked here for months," the sister reminded her brother.

"But I saw him," the brother said. "He looked so pale and ill, and he stared at me so."

"What was he wearing?" the sister asked suspiciously.

The brother answered that Blaney had his sleeves rolled up and had on a large green apron, which he commonly wore when he worked in the house.

Later that day, the sister asked one of the housemaids whether John Blaney had returned to work.

"Didn't you hear, miss," the maid said, much surprised, "that he died this morning?"

In fact, as it turned out, he had died two hours before the brother had seen him.

Why John Blaney appeared only to the brother cannot be explained. For some reason, Blaney's ghost made its presence known and then vanished, never to be seen again. Blaney may have wanted to tell the brother that he had died and appeared to him as he looked at the moment of his death.

A similar episode was reported to Dr. Louisa Rhine by a woman who remembered her encounter as a young girl with the ghost of her grandfather. On December 31, 1926, near Dover, Kansas, the girl was drying the dinner dishes while her mother washed. Suddenly, she saw her grandfather standing outside the kitchen window looking in. He wore his long black overcoat and held a lantern in his hand. He smiled at her.

"There's Grandfather," the girl exclaimed, surprised because he lived twenty-seven miles from their farm.

Her mother saw him as well and said, "Why, it's Dad!"

They ran to the door to bring him inside where it was warm, but he was nowhere to be found. They circled the house looking for him. When they didn't find him, they went back inside and continued their chores. They weren't concerned because the grandfather was well

known as a prankster and was probably playing a trick on them.

The next morning, on their way to Topeka to do some shopping, they were met by the girl's uncle, who flagged down their car.

"Did you hear about Dad yet?" the uncle asked the girl's mother. "He died last night."

As the girl discovered, he had died at the same time that she had seen him standing outside the window. As she told Dr. Rhine many years later, "I am not superstitious, but what I saw was *not imagination*."

Another ghost of the dying was reported to the American Society for Psychical Research by Jessie Sabin in 1908. Mrs. Sabin, in fact, had originally written about the ghost for the *Chicago Daily Journal,* which had sponsored a contest for true ghost stories.

She reported that, on a warm afternoon some years before, her uncle, Israel Slee, was in his office taking a short nap. His office was in a majestic room with floor-to-ceiling windows, which were open because of the heat that day. When Mr. Slee woke up, he must have been momentarily confused because he stepped out one of the windows and fell twenty feet. As he lay on the sidewalk, near death, he repeated the name of his fiancée, "Margaret . . . Margaret . . . Margaret . . ."

Margaret Guines herself was a mile away, having her wedding gown fitted. Standing in front of the dressmaker's mirror, she saw Israel's accident reflected in the mirror.

"Oh, save him, save him! He's falling, dying, he's calling my name!" she screamed.

Then she collapsed, but before she was revived, a messenger brought news of the accident. A few weeks later, Margaret died, apparently from the shock of Israel's tragedy.

Although Mrs. Sabin was a child at the time of her uncle's death and was not present in Margaret's fitting room, her account was verified by her sister. The *Daily Journal* was impressed: her story was awarded first prize in the contest.

IN Memory of
Mr. ISRAEL SLEE
who died
1908
R.I.P.

3. . . . And More Ghosts

Ghost Type 4: *Ghosts of the dead who "talk"*

Although fewer in number, certain ghosts try to communicate a message. They often need help in some way, usually because they have unfinished business. Therefore, they resort to "talking" or using ESP to deliver their message. Why they select particular people to ask for help is not always clear. Maybe some people can receive messages from ghosts while others cannot.

One example of this phenomenon occurred in 1952 to a woman named Mrs. Harrison, who was visiting London, England, and who decided to attend church one Sunday morning. Although a ghost did not appear physically, the ghost of a dead woman communicated with her that morning. The spirit guided Mrs. Harrison to the front of the church, even though she couldn't see any empty seats there.

"Here," Mrs. Harrison heard a voice say inside her head as she walked toward the front of the church. She saw an empty seat next to an old man and sat down.

As the church service began, she closed her eyes for a moment. In her mind, she saw a picture of a beautiful white house with green shutters. Then she heard the voice again: "You must tell him." At that, Mrs. Harrison opened her eyes and realized that she was supposed to tell the old man next to her.

Sure that she was going crazy, she closed her eyes again and immediately saw another vivid picture in her mind, this time of a lush tropical garden.

"You must tell him," she heard the voice say.

Now something even stranger happened. As Mrs. Harrison later reported, "I seemed to change into another person. I could feel that it was no longer me sitting there, but an older, smaller woman. I . . . was especially conscious of a large oval cameo brooch with two dancing Greek figures." The brooch seemed to be pinned to her dress and looked so real that she reached to touch it, but no brooch was there.

"You must tell him!" the voice demanded. "It was my mother's brooch."

The strange feeling passed, and Mrs. Harrison sat through the rest of the church service, occasionally helping the old man next to her find his place in the hymn book. But at the end of the service, she heard the voice again, this time sounding frantic: "You still have time. You must tell him!"

Mrs. Harrison looked toward the old man now, but his seat was empty. Then she saw him walking in a crowd of people toward the door. She rose from her seat and made her way toward the main door of the church. There, she saw that the old man was waiting as the churchgoers streamed past him.

"Thank you for your kindness," he told Mrs. Harrison as she approached him.

"I am so glad you have spoken to me," she replied, "because I wanted to speak to you." Then she described the picture of the white house that had suddenly come into her mind at the beginning of the service.

"I know that house," he said. "It was in the Philippine Islands. I used to live there with my wife."

She told him to say no more, then described the garden scene that had appeared in her mind next. She followed that with a description of the woman who had taken her place and of the brooch that seemed to appear on her dress.

"That was my wife's brooch," the man said. "It belonged to her mother before her. And the garden is my present garden in South Africa." He continued to explain that his wife had died there the previous December after a serious illness.

"You've made me a happy man," he told her. "Now I know my wife is waiting for me. One day soon I will join her again." He touched the lapel of his lightweight suit and added, "This suit is much too thin for English weather, and, as I was leaving my hotel this morning, I turned to go back upstairs to change my overcoat when I distinctly heard my wife's voice say, 'You've no time. You'll be late for church. You *must* go to church this morning.' Now I know why I had to go to church today."

Even though the wife's ghost never appeared physically to Mrs. Harrison, she had no trouble communicating her message. Her wishes were carried out when Mrs. Harrison spoke to the old man. Why the woman's ghost chose Mrs. Harrison over everyone else in the church is a mystery. Also puzzling is why the wife's ghost could not speak directly to the husband. It may be that Mrs. Harrison had some special knack for answering a ghostly call.

A more frightening incident was reported by ghost-hunter Louisa Rhine in 1957. A woman, whose identity was never revealed, lived next door to Mr. and Mrs. Brown, a young couple with three children. Mrs. Brown was mechanically inclined and liked to work on cars, so her husband bought her an old Ford that had to be cranked to start it. She loved the car and spent a lot of time tinkering with it. A month later, however, her appendix ruptured, but her condition was misdiagnosed at first. When it was finally discovered, she could not be saved, and she died while crying out for some water.

Two weeks after her death, the neighbor woman woke in the middle of the night and somehow felt compelled to look out her bedroom window. From there she saw Mrs. Brown's ghost — in this case, white and transparent — cranking her Ford. Quickly, the neighbor called to her husband, who joined her at the window. He saw the ghost as well, as it kept cranking the engine.

The woman decided not to tell Mr. Brown about his wife's ghost, but the next night he came to see his neighbors on his own.

"I wanted to tell you that I'm going to have to move," he told them. The couple were surprised, but they sensed that he had more to say. "I hope you don't think I'm crazy, but I can't stay in the house anymore. My wife's ghost keeps appearing to me," he explained. "I wake up in the middle of the night, and there she is by my bed. She keeps saying, 'If you love me, you'll give me some water. Please . . . just a little water. I'm so thirsty. Please.' I can't take it anymore." A week later Mr. Brown and his children moved.

What's interesting about this case is the fact that Mrs. Brown's ghost was seen by more than one person, although it was seen repeatedly by just the husband. The ghost had a wish, however, that the husband could not fulfill. Rather than try to help his wife understand why her request was impossible to grant, he chose to leave. Whether his wife's ghost followed him was never reported, but she was never seen by the neighbors again.

Ghost Type 5: *Ghosts of the living*

Although this kind of ghost may seem "less ghostly" than the other kinds, some scientists believe that almost one third of the ghosts seen are ghosts of living people. Living ghosts may be relatives or close friends who are seen at times when they are physically in some other location.

For example, on April 13, 1896, a doctor in Anaheim, California, named William Lochman was writing a letter to an old friend who lived in Illinois. As he wrote, the doctor's wife, who was very ill, called her husband from the next room.

"Would you bring me a drink of water, William?" she asked.

As he walked through the dining room to the kitchen, the woman friend to whom he had been writing suddenly appeared standing directly in front of him. She seemed to be looking past him, smiling at the far wall. The doctor took note of her dress, which was brown and yellow plaid and made from what was called basket cloth. The woman's ghost then vanished, but the doctor wrote to tell her what he had seen.

The woman replied sometime later: "I enclose to you a sample of the cloth of the dress which you saw me wear . . . and while I am unable to say where I was or what I was doing at the time . . . I undoubtedly wore the dress on that day, as it is a favorite garment and one which I wear very often, especially in cool weather."

Why did Dr. Lochman see his friend's ghost — especially when he hadn't seen her for sixteen years? There seems to be no real reason for her appearance, which is true for many living ghosts.

Another episode of a living ghost, this time more frightening, happened in 1924 to a man named Watson, who owned a small hotel. Mr. Watson awoke from an afternoon nap in Room 4 and saw a man there. The visitor, whom Mr. Watson did not recognize, ignored him and looked only at the bed. Mr. Watson could feel that something was wrong with the man and kept staring at his face. Then, he happened to glance down and see that there was nothing below the man's knees. Mr. Watson was about to yell for help when the man faded away. That night, Mr. Watson moved out of Room 4, but as the weeks passed, he thought little more of his strange experience.

Seven weeks later, a man came to the hotel and asked for a room. Mr. Watson immediately thought that the man looked familiar.

"Haven't you stayed here before, sir?" he asked.

"No," the man answered. His name was O'Toole, he told Mr. Watson, and he had been living in Australia for the past fifteen years.

Mr. Watson shrugged and registered him for Room 3. The man paid for the room and left for the evening.

The next morning, the hotel maid knocked on Mr. Watson's door.

"No one answers in Room 4," she told him.

"It wasn't occupied last night," he said. It had been a slow night, and only Rooms 1, 2, and 3 were occupied.

"But Room 3 is vacant," she said. "And the door to Room 4 is locked."

At that, Mr. Watson went with the maid to Room 4 and unlocked the door. Inside, he saw that someone was in the bed with the covers over his face. Thankful that the maid was with him, he pulled back the covers and found the cold, white body of Mr. O'Toole, his eyes staring blankly at the ceiling.

Only then did Mr. Watson realize where he had seen the man before. He was the ghost in Room 4 seven weeks earlier.

In a case like this, the living ghost may have been a signal of death, even though the death was not to occur until weeks later. Still, nothing about Mr. Watson's experience with the ghost indicated that O'Toole was going to die.

Ghost Type 6: *Poltergeists — invisible, playful ghosts*

Poltergeists are "noisy spirits" who haunt individuals or families, not the houses they live in. They are always found indoors and almost always cause trouble. Poltergeists are likely to move objects, sometimes breaking them. They may hurl vases from mantels or move heavy pieces of furniture in front of astonished observers. Some say that poltergeists are not ghosts — just strange events that may be caused by a young person in a family living under a great deal of tension. A troubled young person may be able to create a powerful energy force that carries out the poltergeist's activities. Still, other people believe that poltergeists are ghosts who enjoy mischief.

The case of Virginia Campbell, which occurred in Sauchie, Scotland, in 1960, helps to explain why scientists disagree about poltergeists.

In October 1960, Virginia, an eleven-year-old schoolgirl, moved from Ireland to Scotland. She was upset that her father had to stay behind to sell their farm. Then her mother found work in another town, and Virginia had to

38

live with her aunt and uncle in Sauchie. Worst of all, she had to leave behind her beloved dog, Toby. So Virginia, who was a shy girl anyway, was left to stay with her uncle's family, share a bed with her cousin Margaret, and start school in a new town.

The first major sign of poltergeist activity happened on November 23, when some strange knocking was heard shortly after Virginia and Margaret had gone to bed. Even after Margaret ran terrified from the bedroom, the knocking continued. At first, her aunt and uncle thought that Virginia was making the knocking sounds, but when the knocks persisted, they called a local minister, who determined that she was not. As the minister watched, a large, heavy linen chest that stood near Virginia's bed began to rock back and forth. It rose off the floor and moved toward the bed before it returned to its original position. When it had stopped, the minister and a neighbor moved the chest to the hallway for fear that it might hurt Virginia if it moved again.

Some of the most astonishing events were seen by Virginia's teacher. On November 25, Virginia was seated in front of an empty desk in her classroom. Much to the teacher's surprise, she saw the desk rise slowly upward until it was an inch off the floor. It stayed there for a moment, then gently lowered itself back to the floor. The teacher rushed over to make sure that strings hadn't been used to raise the desk. She found it to be an ordinary desk; there was no way to explain its movement.

Three days later, on November 28, the teacher was again surprised when Virginia approached her desk. A blackboard pointer on the teacher's desk began to vibrate and roll until it fell on the floor. As the pointer moved, the teacher noticed that her desk was vibrating as well. Then the desk began to rotate away from the teacher. She looked at Virginia, who was still standing a few feet away. At that point, Virginia started to cry and said she hadn't done anything.

Was the Sauchie poltergeist a ghost or was it a series of uncanny events caused by Virginia? Some observers thought that Virginia's unhappiness about moving and leaving her dog behind was responsible for the haunting. At any rate, Toby was eventually returned to Virginia, and, by March 1961, the poltergeist activity ceased.

Until scientists know more, perhaps the best way to think about poltergeists is that they are probably the most dangerous type of ghost. If you're lucky enough to find one, you will want to be careful because their mischief can sometimes be harmful. Some poltergeists have been known to bite people or throw heavy objects at them. Remember, any ghost that can throw furniture should be treated with care.

These six ghost types are the most common kinds of ghosts. If you accidentally meet one, you will want to know which kind you have met. That way you will prove what an expert ghosthunter you are.

If you set out to find a ghost, though, you will probably have luck finding only three of the six types: a ghost of the dead who has been seen repeatedly, a ghost of the dead who has been seen only a few times, or a poltergeist. You can't decide to find the other three types of ghosts; they'll decide when they're going to meet you. For that reason, most of the ghost stories in this book are about the three kinds you might find if you start your own ghost hunt.

4. Beginning Your Ghost Hunt

Before you can find a ghost, you need to know where to look. If you're like most people, cemeteries are the first places you'd think of looking. This is another mistaken idea about ghosts, because only a few ghosts can be found in cemeteries.

A small English town in Kent claims to have a Red Lady who haunts its churchyard cemetery. The woman, who is dressed in red, has been seen there searching for the grave of her baby. Supposedly, her child died at birth. For whatever reason, its burial was done quickly and secretly, and its grave was never marked. The woman died later, still grieving for her dead child. As you can see, this ghost had a reason to haunt a cemetery. Most ghosts of the dead, though, have no connection to the place they were buried. They are much more likely to haunt the places they knew when they were alive.

43

The most obvious place to begin your search for ghosts is in a haunted house. But before you look down the street, you should look at your own house or apartment: *could it be haunted?* Here's a checklist of questions you'll need to answer to determine if your house or apartment is haunted.

 # 1. Do you live in an old house?

Haunted houses are usually old buildings. That's because, over the years, more people have lived and died there. Maybe one of them became a ghost. Of course, most houses — even the oldest ones — are not haunted, so the age of a house doesn't guarantee that you'll find a ghost.

Even if you live in a new house, don't give up hope. While no one may have lived there before you, it's possible for a poltergeist to make its presence known. You can also be visited anywhere by a ghost of the dying or a ghost of the living.

One family in Ireland, for example, was the first to occupy a new house, only to find that it was haunted. The family heard knocking sounds throughout the house. One night, after everyone had gone to bed, the parents heard loud knocking at their bedroom door. When they called for the person to come in, no one entered, and when the father finally opened the door, no one was there. The next day, the family received a telegram informing them that the mother's brother had died the night before — at almost the same time the knocking had occurred. Perhaps the ghost of the uncle, unable to appear visually, knocked to indicate that he had died. Or it may be that the family was haunted by a poltergeist.

In another case, reported by ghost researchers Gerald Solfvin and Fred Matthews, a family in New Bedford, Massachusetts, lived in a haunted house, but when they moved the haunting continued, both in their old house and in their new one. Mrs. Sullivan and her three great-grandsons lived in the upstairs portion of a small house that had been divided into two apartments. Downstairs lived Mr. Crane, an old man who did not get along well with Mrs. Sullivan.

Sometime during the spring of 1974, Mr. Crane told his son, "If it's possible, I'm going to come back and haunt her after I die." A few months later, in August, he died, and a Mrs. Turnbull and her three-year-old son moved into his apartment. Shortly afterward, Mrs. Sullivan began to hear footsteps and the thud of a cane, as if an old man were walking through the house. Chairs squeaked, a rocker on the front porch rocked, doorknobs rattled, and the mailbox opened and closed — when no one but a ghost could have been responsible. Mrs. Sullivan never discussed the noises with Mrs. Turnbull, but she had heard them, too. What's more, Mrs. Turnbull had also heard loud breathing sounds one day, as if someone were standing beside her.

In January 1975, Mrs. Sullivan and her great-grandsons moved to another building. There, during a six-week period, researchers who had been called in to investigate counted 184 inexplicable incidents. The boys' toy soldiers whirled in the air; a rocking chair tipped over sideways several times. Perhaps the most frightening aspect of this haunting was the use of the family's gas stove. Without warning, an object would fly toward the stove. As the object approached, the burners would ignite and burn it. Researchers concluded that a poltergeist was responsible, since no ghost was ever seen.

But a poltergeist was not responsible for the haunting that continued at the Sullivans' old apartment. In fact, shortly after they left, a middle-aged couple moved in upstairs. In the middle of their second night there, they packed their things and moved out, forfeiting a month's rent. They never reported what they saw or heard.

A month later, Mrs. Turnbull's downstairs apartment was robbed one night when she was out of town. Because many valuables were left behind, the responding police officers thought the burglars might return to finish the job, so they decided to hide in the house until morning if necessary to catch the thieves. Then the officers, who knew nothing about the haunting, began to hear strange noises in the otherwise empty house. They left and spent the rest of the night safely parked in their car down the street. When asked by researchers why they had left the scene, the officer in charge replied that the noises in the house had bothered them; he thought that the house had been infested with rats. As the researchers knew, that house showed no evidence of rats.

Although the robbers never returned, the ghost did. A few weeks later, the upstairs apartment was rented again, this time to two young women with preschool children. One of the women, a Ms. Davenport, reported that she had been pinched. She also said that her three-year-old son watched a ghost walk into the bathroom. He asked his mother who the man was, but when she replied that she hadn't seen anyone, the boy became frightened and began to cry.

Several months later, when the upstairs apartment was vacant again, another woman moved in and experienced many of the same happenings. In December 1975, she tried to communicate with the ghost and, as she told Solfvin and Matthews, felt that she succeeded. From then on, the ghost bothered her much less often.

2. Have you heard any noises that you can't explain?

Maybe you've heard footsteps and creaking when no one in the house could have made the sounds. Sometimes loud banging is heard in haunted houses. The important thing is to make sure that the sounds could not have been made by anyone or anything else. Could someone in your family be playing a trick on you?

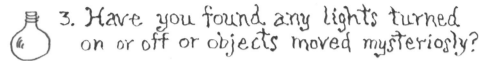

3. Have you found any lights turned on or off or objects moved mysteriosly?

Sometimes lights go on unaccountably in haunted houses. A ghost may have turned on the light switch, but it's also possible that someone else did it after you left the room. Ghosts, especial.y poltergeists, have also been known to move pictures or furniture. For example, if a picture keeps falling off the wall, perhaps a poltergeist in the house doesn't care for your taste in art — or else you need a stronger nail.

One woman named Frances Freeman had this problem when she bought a three-bedroom ranch house in a Bakersfield, California, retirement community in 1981. According to Dr. L. Stafford Betty, who reported the story, the house originally belonged to Meg Lyons, who had lived there from 1962 until her death in 1976. For five years, the house was left undisturbed while Meg's daughter and son-in-law, who inherited the place, tried to decide whether to move into it or sell it. Finally, they chose to sell the house to Mrs. Freeman. Only when Mrs. Freeman began to renovate it did the poltergeist make itself known.

Workmen installed a new kitchen sink and a large cabinet in the place where Meg's dinette had been. As soon as they had gone, Mrs. Freeman began to hear some mysterious thumping and scraping sounds in the kitchen. But she was tired and didn't bother to check; besides, the furnace was on and might have been responsible. The next night, she heard the same sounds but again didn't explore. The following morning, though, she found the drawers of the new kitchen cabinet open.

In fact, for the next two months, the new cabinet drawers were opened repeatedly. Mrs. Freeman even called the carpenter back to make sure the cabinet was level; he assured her it was. Other things began to happen in the house. Doors were opened, lights were turned on.

In one of the strangest incidents, Mrs. Freeman tried repeatedly to hang a photograph of three women taken shortly before the Civil War. On five different mornings, she found the picture removed from its hook and propped against the baseboard. Finally, she felt a "presence" direct her to one of the bedrooms, where she hung the picture next to a light switch. As Mrs. Freeman told Dr. Betty, "I would never have hung it there myself. It was much too low and too close to the light switch, but I felt myself directed to hang it there." From then on, though, the picture remained where Mrs. Freeman had hung it.

This incident confirmed that the poltergeist was probably Meg Lyons, for shortly after the picture was hung, Meg's son-in-law, Luke, visited Mrs. Freeman. She gave him a tour of the house, pointing out how she had redecorated. When she showed him the bedroom that displayed the photograph, Luke was stunned. Meg had had a similar photograph, and it had been hung in exactly the same place. Furthermore, Meg was much shorter than Mrs. Freeman, which explained why the picture had been hung so low. Was Meg trying to communicate to Luke? Or was she trying to keep her house looking as it always had?

Finally, on January 25, 1982, Mrs. Freeman made the mistake of buying paint and wallpaper to redo the master bedroom — Meg's old bedroom! Since she was tired, Mrs. Freeman left the materials on the new kitchen counter and went to bed. A few hours later, Mrs. Freeman heard pounding and crashing noises, as if someone were tearing the kitchen apart. Eventually, the noises stopped and Mrs. Freeman fell asleep.

In the middle of the night, however, she woke up and made her way to the bathroom. As she washed her hands in the sink, the bathroom window slid open. Mrs. Freeman couldn't see anyone outside the window, so she quickly closed it and hurried back to her bedroom. There, the bedroom window slammed shut at the same time that the bathroom window slid open again. Then her closet doors began to open and close wildly.

50

"I've got to get out of here, this is just too much," she told herself.

Mrs. Freeman was so certain that her life was in danger that she left the house that night, dressed in a nightgown and coat. Only when two sensitives — people who believe that they have the ability to feel or see a ghost — visited the house and asked Meg's ghost to leave did all of Meg's shenanigans cease.

4. Are you aware of any unexpected drafts of cold air?

People living in a haunted house often report a coldness in a certain room or area of the house. If this happened during the winter, you would probably not be surprised. But if you felt a blast of cold air on a hot summer's afternoon — and there was no air conditioner nearby — you might have reason to suspect a ghost.

5. Have you ever felt that someone was in the room with you when you were alone?

Some people who have lived in haunted houses have sensed a "presence" in the room with them, even though they couldn't see anyone. This presence may have been a ghost.

As a good ghosthunter, you should be able to get a feeling when you walk into a house about whether a ghost might be present. Haunted houses are said to have a certain atmosphere. Their air may seem different from the air in ordinary houses. Your skin may prickle or feel clammy as you walk through. Trust your suspicions. If you feel the presence of a ghost, you can set out to meet it.

But sensing a presence alone does not mean that a ghost haunts your house. One woman told a ghost-hunting college professor named Gertrude Schmeidler, on March 24, 1 5, that she thought her house was haunted. The house, whose location was never revealed, was sixty years old, and the woman, whose name was never reported, had lived there for five years. Within the last two and a half years, though, she had become aware of someone's presence in the house. This feeling occurred many different times during the day, but only in certain parts of the house.

Although she had never seen or heard the ghost, she was sure that it was a man, perhaps forty-five years old, who was a little shy and anxious but otherwise gentle. Even though he did not seem harmful, he frightened the woman anyway. One day, when she was playing the piano, she had felt his presence so much that she ran outdoors.

Her daughter also felt the ghost in the same places. Then, when her son mentioned that he felt something in

52

the house, too, she contacted Professor Schmeidler, who volunteered to find out if the house was haunted. She asked nine sensitives to visit the house separately. If a ghost was present, Professor Schmeidler was sure that the sensitives would locate it. Unfortunately, only two sensitives could locate two of the ten areas of the house where the family had felt the ghost. Another sensitive could not find any sign of haunting. When she toured the house, she said that the woman who owned the house might have made up the ghost herself for some unconscious reason.

What do you think? Did the ghost exist or not? No one ever saw it, and no one ever heard it. It wasn't a poltergeist, since it never moved any furniture or turned on any lights. Maybe it wasn't real, except in the woman's mind.

If you think that your house or apartment is haunted, it will most likely be haunted by a ghost who has some connection with the place you live. For that reason, you will want to find out about any former residents. You or someone in your family should be able to visit the local government office in which real estate deeds are recorded, to look up the names of the people who have owned your house. Or, if you have a friendly landlord, you may be able to find out the names of former tenants. Then you may want to interview your neighbors about the former residents. What kind of people were they? Did anything strange ever happen in your house? Did anyone ever die there? The more you know about the previous occupants, the more ready you'll be to find a ghost, if one is there to be found.

Mrs. Wood, a woman who lived in a haunted apartment house in Brooklyn, New York, from 1894 to 1898, researched her building's history. As she reported to the American Society for Psychical Research in 1920, the previous tenant, Mr. Hammond, "had died there two months before we took the house. He died in the back parlor as had everybody else who had died there so far as we could discover; and a good many had died there. The house was about thirty-five years old at that time. We had heard about Mr. Hammond's peculiar and pathetic illness."

In fact, Mrs. Wood later discovered from her neighbor, Mrs. Marion, that Mr. Hammond had been "perfectly green" before he died and delirious much of the time.

Next, try to learn something about the history of the building itself. Was it ever remodeled so that the floor plans were changed? Were any fireplaces or doors ever bricked up and closed off? Are there any secret rooms? In this way, if you do see a ghost walking through your dining room wall, say, you will already know that fifty years earlier, a door used to be there; the ghost just walked through a door that no longer exists. Knowing this will help you decide how old the ghost is and who it might be. Or, if a secret room is present, maybe the ghost haunts your house because his body was never buried but merely hidden in the room.

Of course, even if you learn about all of the people who used to live in your house, and even if some fireplaces were bricked up, and even if someone died there, it may not be haunted. In that case, you may want to ask your friends and neighbors whether they know of any haunted houses. Sometimes neighbors know a lot about which houses have ghost stories connected to them. What's more, your neighbors may have seen a ghost, or witnessed some supernatural events, in their own homes. If you're lucky, maybe you'll get invited in.

If your house isn't haunted and if your friends and neighbors haven't been any help, don't give up hope. The next chapter will describe the second-best place to look for ghosts.

5. Digging Up Local Ghosts

The second-best place to begin your ghost hunt is a place you might not consider: the main branch of your local library. You probably won't find a real ghost there, but you'll get a lot of help about where to look for ghosts in your town.

If your town has a small library, ask the librarian if there is a Ghost File. This folder will contain all of the articles that were written about ghosts in your area. If you live in a large city, the main branch of the library probably has a local history room, where you will find information about local ghosts. If you know how to use the card catalogue in that room, you can look up the heading "Ghosts." Old newspaper and magazine articles about your city and its surrounding area may be listed in a special index. Your librarian can tell you if such an index exists. Write down the articles you want, and the librarian will either get them for you or show you how to find them yourself. The local history room may even have its own Ghost File that you can look through.

If you can't find any information, check with the librarian. Say that you'd like to know what material the library has about local ghosts. Your librarian will probably come up with some information, even if it has to be requested from another, larger library.

Something to keep in mind, as you find articles about ghosts and hauntings, is that ghosts of the dead don't necessarily haunt the place where they died. What may surprise you is that some ghosts haunt places that they never even lived in or visited when they were alive.

An excellent example of this was the haunting of a two-family house, just three years old, in Pittsburgh, Pennsylvania. From August 1971 to April 1972, the two families who lived there witnessed a number of eerie incidents. The Cramers, who lived upstairs, reported that lights and radios were switched on and off without explanation. They also observed a white, misty figure in different rooms of their apartment. Their downstairs neighbors, the Henrys, also saw a misty figure. Like the Cramers, they also heard a child's laughter on more than one occasion.

In one of the more frightening experiences, Mr. and Mrs. Henry had just gone to bed when they felt a small, childlike body get into bed between them. Because it was dark, they couldn't see the figure clearly, but they

knew that their own children were fast asleep. Then the body left the bed and ran around the room, moving objects and laughing mischievously. Mrs. Henry admitted that the child's laughter was "beautiful, but it scared me."

A writer for a local newspaper who studied the case concluded that the ghost was that of a nine-year-old mentally retarded boy who had been killed in an accident just before his mother had moved into the house. The child never lived in the house — and his mother no longer lived there when he began to haunt it. Nonetheless, the child managed to haunt the two families who resided there. As you can see, this ghost had no particular reason to haunt the house once his mother had moved away.

During your library search, you should look for three different kinds of ghost information: places, people, and days that are haunted.

Step 1: *Finding haunted places*

Haunted houses. Besides your own house, you should try to find others that may be haunted. Usually, every large town has at least one house that was reported to be haunted at one time or another. Your library's local history room is the best place to investigate which houses in your town are said to be haunted. Sometimes old, stately houses become museums that you can tour; the museum may have its own ghost story. Guides in such places usually know whether a ghost has been seen in the house.

Even when you find a number of houses that are (or were) haunted, you may have some problems visiting them. First, you will need the owner's permission to be allowed into the house. The owner may not want any ghosthunters tramping through. Also, many of the best haunted houses are no longer standing, especially if they were too haunted to live in.

One house that was so haunted it had to be torn down was Hinton Ampner, which was located in a town southwest of London. Exactly why the house was haunted is unknown, but there are reports that a baby was mur-

60

dered there around 1740. About twenty-five years later, the house was inherited by the Ricketts family. Since they had moved to England from Jamaica, they didn't know much about the place. Still, before long they discovered the truth: the house was quite haunted. The sound of doors slamming was constant, even after new locks were put on the doors. They saw two ghosts at different times: a gentleman and a tall woman, both dressed in drab clothes.

The noises continued during the years that the Ricketts family lived in the house. Sometimes the noises were pleasant, like the sound of music playing; at other times, they were terrifying. The family heard groaning, yelling, and shrieks. Finally, they heard the sound of gunshots night after night. Of course, they could find no explanation for any of the noises. Six years after they moved in, they decided that Hinton Ampner was unfit for humans and moved to another house. For a few years, the place was deserted, then it was torn down. As the workmen ripped it apart, they found a small skull under the floorboards in one of the rooms. Was it the skull of the child who had been murdered? Was the skull even related to the haunting? No one knew for sure, but when another house named Hinton Ampner was built on the same site, the haunting never recurred.

Besides haunted houses, there are other places that may be haunted in your town. Try your library's Ghost File to see whether any of the following places in your area have ghosts.

Historical public buildings. Sometimes a building that is historically important itself or near a site of historical importance will be haunted. In Europe, the building might be a castle or a church. In the United States, it could be a government building or even a school.

One such site is at Nebraska Wesleyan University in Lincoln, where, on October 3, 1963, Mrs. Coleen Baterbaugh had an extraordinary experience. She not only saw a ghost, but for a few moments she was transported back in time.

Mrs. Baterbaugh was on an errand for the dean, Sam Dahl, when she entered a room in one of the university's oldest buildings. Instantly, she became aware of a strong, musty odor permeating the room. She stopped in her tracks and immediately sensed the presence of some-

62

one else. At the same time, all of the usual noises and activity in a university building ceased, creating a deathly silence. Mrs. Baterbaugh looked through a window into an adjacent room and saw a woman who seemed to be reaching toward one of the shelves of a cabinet. But the woman wasn't moving, and Mrs. Baterbaugh realized that what she saw was an apparition. In a moment, the woman faded away.

But Mrs. Baterbaugh's ghostly experience wasn't over yet. Suddenly, she sensed another presence, this time a man. When she looked, no one was visible. Still, she felt that he was sitting at a desk nearby. His ghost did not materialize, but something more frightening did. As she stared at the desk, Mrs. Baterbaugh happened to glance out the window behind it. Normally, she would have seen a busy, modern university campus. But nothing modern was visible: the main street wasn't there and neither was Willard House, a new campus building. She realized that the ghost had not come to her time; rather, she had gone back to his. Instinctively, she ran out of the room to the hall, where everything returned to normal.

Ghosthunter D. Scott Rogo explains that instead of only seeing a ghost (the usual experience), Mrs. Baterbaugh found herself inhabiting the ghost's time and place; she became part of the past for a few moments. With a little research, Rogo discovered that the ghost Mrs. Baterbaugh had witnessed could be accounted for. Twenty-seven years earlier, Clarissa Mills, a music professor, died in a room in the same building. Exactly why Mrs. Baterbaugh was able to go back in time and experience Professor Mills's ghost and return is unknown. This makes it one of the most unusual hauntings ever reported.

The haunting of another historical building took place at the New York State capitol in Albany, according to journalist Lawrence Cortesi. The west wing of the building was destroyed by fire on March 29, 1911, claiming the life of Samuel J. Abbott, the night watchman. In the search for his remains in the smoldering ashes of the building, all that was found were his belt buckle and his boots.

The New York State Capitol

Sometime later, the ghost of Samuel Abbott began to haunt the capitol during late-night hours, especially the legislative assembly chamber on the fifth floor, and it continued to do so until the end of October 1981. During the 1970s, janitors, maintenance workers, and security guards all seemed to have had some encounter with the ghost that they identified as "George." The sounds of heavy breathing, jangling keys, and turning doorknobs scared more than one employee and caused several to request transfers to other floors; however, some brave souls chose to remain.

One custodian heard furniture being moved on the sixth floor during her shift every night, even though she knew that no furniture was on the sixth floor and that no one was working there anyway. Rather than request a transfer, she started carrying a radio so she wouldn't hear any odd sounds.

Ann Fisher, an Albany woman who specialized in studying supernatural happenings, arranged to hold a séance in the assembly chamber on Halloween night, 1981, accompanied by a group of students and two skeptical television reporters who agreed to film the event.

"Samuel Abbott, please come to us because we have a special message for you," Ms. Fisher said at the start of the séance.

In a moment, a blast of cold air blew through the chamber. Then, without warning, one of the television camera lights went out. One reporter, Frank Cirilli, quickly changed bulbs, while the other, Bryan Jackson, examined a nearby radiator to see whether it had stopped working and caused the cold air. As you can probably imagine, the radiator was working quite nicely.

"You are now in our presence, Samuel Abbott, and you may leave now. Your agony is ended; go where you must go," Ann Fisher continued.

Her statement was followed by another gust of cold air and the extinguishing of another camera light. Finally, two loud bangs shook the room, though nothing apparent caused them.

Shortly, Ann Fisher announced the end of the séance. Everyone in the chamber, except the reporters, swore that they felt the ghost's presence. However, the reporters inadvertently helped to prove the existence of Samuel Abbott's ghost.

Back at their studio, Cirilli and Jackson were surprised to discover the results of their work. First, when the light bulbs that had gone out were tested, both lit up normally. This was unusual, since bulbs that go out are almost always bad. Second, when the reporters played the soundtrack of the séance, they expected to hear the two loud bangs that had startled everyone near the end. Instead, they were perplexed to find that every part of the séance except the bangs was recorded on the tape. Finally, and most telling, as the reporters watched the film for the first time, they saw the greenish, misty out-

66

line of a human figure above the séance table — an image that no one in the assembly chamber had seen that night.

Thanks to Ann Fisher, visitors to the Albany capitol these days who want to see Samuel Abbott's ghost will be disappointed, for they will enter a building that is no longer haunted. Other buildings with similar histories may still have their own ghosts; a thorough investigation may give you some ideas.

Battlefields. Other historical sites worth checking are battlefields. These would include French and Indian War, Revolutionary War, and Civil War battlefields. Many people have reported seeing or hearing ghosts — and sometimes entire armies of ghosts — on the sites of former battles.

Two women on a trip to Dieppe, France, in 1951 heard ghostly battle sounds on the ninth anniversary of an important World War II battle. The women, who were awakened around 4 A.M. on August 4, wrote separate accounts of what they had heard that morning. Both described "cries and shouts and gunfire" and "dive bombing." They heard bombshells at the same moment. The sounds stopped at 4:50 A.M., but began again at 5:30. Ten minutes later, after intense bombing, the noise ended again. This happened twice more, until seven o'clock that morning, when all of the sounds ceased.

Both of the women were surprised that the loud noises had not awakened anyone else staying in their vacation house. When the others awoke, sometime after seven, the women asked them whether they had heard any unusual noises, but no one had. What they realized, as they did further research, was that the hours that they heard the sounds of the battle corresponded almost exactly to the time of the real battle at Dieppe.

Roads and highways. Everyone has heard the story of the phantom hitchhiker who gets a ride from a driver, asks to be let off at a house, and then forgets to take his hat or his jacket. When the driver tries to return the hitchhiker's belongings, he discovers that the hitchhiker has been dead for many years. Every year, on the anniversary of his death, he hitches a ride home. But this story is probably fictitious.

Here's a true incident, reported by Andrew Green, that happened on the south coast of England on June 14, 1979. As twenty-two-year-old Robert Hove drove along a main road, he approached a crosswalk. Seeing no one there, he did not stop. Suddenly, an old lady in a dirty brown coat appeared in the middle of the crosswalk and stepped in front of his car. He couldn't stop the car in time; he heard a horrible thud as it hit the woman. Stunned, he got out to see whether she might be alive, but as he bent down to look under his front fender, he could not find her. Then he noticed that another driver,

68

who had been traveling in the opposite direction at the time of the accident, had stopped and was shaking his head.

"What happened?" Mr. Hove asked the other driver.

"I've just hit an old woman," he replied, "but she seems to have vanished."

They talked a moment and came to the conclusion that they had both hit the same woman: she had white hair, a pleated skirt, red shoes, and walked with a noticeable stoop. Then they asked some onlookers whether they had seen the old woman, but no one except the two drivers had seen anything.

Confused by what had happened, they decided to go to the police station to report the accident. There, an officer told them that an elderly woman had been knocked down and killed in the same place in 1959. He said that the police received several reports on the same day every few years.

"Don't worry about it," the officer said. "There are always two drivers who report the incident."

Step 2: *Finding a haunted person*

Like Virginia Campbell in Sauchie, Scotland, some people are prone to having poltergeist experiences. They — and not their homes — are haunted. During your library hunt, you can look for information about poltergeist hauntings that have occurred in your town. If one was reported, does that person still live there? If she does, would you be able to contact her?

Perhaps you attend school with someone who is having a poltergeist experience. All of the reports about Virginia Campbell and her strange behavior in school indicate that her classmates never noticed the desk or the pointer moving. As a ghosthunter, you should be on the lookout for unusual events. If you see something odd happening, check it out. Your eyes may have been mistaken. On the other hand, you may have seen a ghost.

Another example of a haunted person is Julio Vasquez, a nineteen-year-old Cuban refugee who worked in a Miami, Florida, warehouse. Julio was a shipping clerk for Tropication Arts, Inc., at 117 NE 54th Street, and from December 1966 to February 1967, he was the center of 224 separate incidents of poltergeist activity. Most of the incidents involved moving or falling objects in the warehouse. Many of the objects were broken as a result. Thirteen times, witnesses saw objects begin to move without any explanation.

Julio was suspected as the "haunted person" simply because he was the only one present when all of the events occurred. However, none of the poltergeist activity "followed him home"; it was only reported at work. When he quit his job at the warehouse in February, all of the activity stopped there.

But it followed Julio to his next job, at a branch of a national shoe store on North Miami Avenue, according to ghosthunter Susy Smith. At first, the incidents were harmless enough; for example, a fire extinguisher somehow fell from its wall mount. Then, more destructive events began to occur. In the back room of the store, jars of dye used to tint customers' shoes were lined up on a table. One day, without warning, the jars began to pop up and shatter on the floor, staining it different colors. Julio was nowhere near the jars, but his boss began to suspect his influence. Needless to say, Julio only lasted a week selling shoes.

The poltergeist haunted Julio through a few more jobs, but seemed to disappear by June 1968, when Julio married. Apparently, poltergeists prefer to remain single.

Step 3: *Finding haunted days*

Like the old woman who suddenly appeared in front of the two drivers on the anniversary of her death, ghosts sometimes haunt places only on a certain day of the year. For that reason, certain dates may be good times to find ghosts, if you know your local history. If an accident or tragedy occurred on a certain day, you might try to visit the site of the event on its anniversary. This may sound like a gruesome idea to all but the most serious ghost-hunter.

One haunting related to a particular date occurs in Bramber, England. The town itself has just one main street with a few shops. Perched on a hill overlooking the town is Bramber Castle, which was a stronghold during the reign of King John at the beginning of the thirteenth century.

The lord of the castle was William de Braose. In order to make sure that de Braose was loyal to him, the king asked the lord to give him custody of his two children. But de Braose and his wife, Matilda, saw things a little differently and refused to give up their children. King John was so angry that he sent soldiers to Bramber Castle to seize the entire family.

Somehow, the family was informed of King John's plans and escaped capture by traveling to Ireland. But the king wasn't to be stopped. He took the family prisoner in Ireland, had them sent back to England, and locked the children in Windsor Castle, where they were starved to death.

Although the date of their deaths is not recorded, it is thought to be Christmas Day. For, on Christmas, two young children have been seen running through Bramber, stopping motorists and pedestrians. The children, who are barefoot and dressed in rags, appear as if they haven't eaten for weeks. They beg everyone they stop for food. Then they disappear.

By the time you're finished looking for ghosts in the library, you should have made a list of a few local ghosts that might still be haunting your town. Then you can decide which one you want to look for first.

6. Ten Ways to Find a Ghost

Now you're ready to begin your ghost hunt. To find a ghost, you must be brave, determined, and, most of all, patient. The hardest part about your hunt is that you'll never know if all of your work helped you find a ghost — until you see one. What's more, you may be the kind of person who isn't able to see ghosts, even if one's standing in front of you.

Scientists are interested in why some people are lucky enough to see ghosts and others aren't. They have studied different ghosts and hauntings, and analyzed where the people were and what they were doing when they saw their ghosts, in order to be able to tell other people how to find a ghost.

As you start your ghost hunt, you may be wondering what your chances are of spotting one. Did you know that many surveys have been done to determine how many people have seen ghosts? One survey of residents in Charlottesville, Virginia, in 1979, indicated that 17 percent of the population claimed to have seen a ghost of one kind or another. On a broader level, a national survey in 1975 found that almost 27 percent of the respondents had been in touch with someone dead, although it was not clear that all 27 percent had seen ghosts. These results *could* mean that one out of every four or five people in the United States has seen a ghost. But a survey would have to be taken of every city in the United States to prove that, and no ghosthunter has had the time or the money to do that yet.

Instead of worrying about your chances, you can increase them yourself by using the following suggestions. From my own research, I have determined that there are at least ten ways that you might find a ghost. These suggestions should improve your chances of meeting one, but keep in mind that some of them will not be easy to follow.

Tip 1: *Start with a place that you're familiar with*

The majority of people see ghosts in or near their own home. If you feel that your house or apartment is haunted, you should start there. Many people also see ghosts in surroundings that are very familiar — like the houses of relatives or friends, or a church. But very few people have seen a ghost while they are at work; maybe that's because a job is a minor part of a person's life. In fact, only about 10 percent of the people who see ghosts see them in unfamiliar places.

If you want to look for a ghost in a haunted house that you've never visited before, try to become familiar with it before you look for ghosts there. Visit the house a number of times. Then, when you feel comfortable there, wait for your ghost.

One woman in Springfield, Ohio, reported seeing a ghost of the living (in this case, her mother) on Christmas Eve, 1904. At six o'clock that night, Frederica Coblentz had just finished decorating the tree when her mother called downstairs and asked her to bring a glass of water to her bedroom. The Coblentz family's house was large enough to have two staircases. As Frederica climbed the rear stairs with the glass of water, she saw her mother descending the front staircase.

"Mother, here is your water," she called, but her mother didn't seem to hear. Frederica followed her down the front stairs.

"Mother, here is your glass of water," she repeated.

Her mother continued walking. Frederica followed her to the front hall. Finally, she said, "Mother, here is your glass of water." When she didn't answer, Frederica continued, "Why on earth don't you take it? Where are you going?"

Just then, her mother turned and entered the darkened parlor. As Frederica watched, her mother walked slowly around the parlor, stopping occasionally as if she was searching for matches to light the gaslights.

"Are you looking for the matches?" Frederica asked.

Suddenly, the outline of her mother's body blurred as if she were moving to a darker part of the room. Then Frederica began to realize that something was wrong. Her mother's form grew fainter and fainter. When it vanished, Frederica was so stunned that the glass of water slipped out of her hand and crashed to the floor. She began to tremble at the thought that she had seen her mother's ghost.

She raced upstairs and found her mother in her bedroom. No one could ever account for this mysterious episode, but it probably could have happened only in the familiar surroundings of Frederica's home.

Tip 2: *Stay indoors*

Most people are indoors when they spy a ghost. For this reason, select a familiar indoor location to begin your ghost hunt.

It is possible, however, to see a ghost outdoors, like one sighting that occurred around 1965 in Los Angeles. A journalist, having tea with the owners of a haunted house one afternoon, was seated on the patio when she saw a man wearing a black suit walk into the area surrounding the swimming pool. The man circled the pool,

78

staring at something in the water. As the journalist turned to ask why she hadn't been introduced to the man, he disappeared. When she described the man to her hosts, they confirmed that she had just seen the ghost that haunted their house. In fact, she had the honor of being the first person to observe the ghost outside, since at least three other sightings had been made indoors.

So it is possible to spot a ghost outdoors. Remember, though, that the ghost was spotted inside the house first.

Tip 3: *Read a book*

If you are staking out a certain ghost's territory, you should take along a good book to read. This may sound like silly advice until you know that many people were reading a book right before they looked up and saw a ghost. It will make more sense when you realize that

when you get "lost" in a book, you are taking your mind off your surroundings. Some scientists think that only by removing yourself from the real world can you see a ghost.

According to a report filed with the British Society for Psychical Research in 1895, one man saw a ghost of the living after he had been reading for twenty minutes or so. The man was sitting in his living room, waiting for two friends to return from a concert, when he became aware that another presence was in the room with him. He knew somehow that one of the friends he was waiting for, Anthony, was standing behind and to the left of him. Without turning his head, the man moved his eyes to the left and saw a leg dressed in a gray material, similar to the pants that Anthony often wore.

The man realized that something was odd. In a moment, he glanced to his left again and saw the full figure of Anthony, standing four feet away from him. He could see Anthony clearly. His face was very pale, his head was thrown slightly back, his eyes were shut. But on one side of his throat, just under his jaw, a bloody wound appeared. Anthony's body remained motionless for a short time, then vanished.

Later, the man discovered that his friend had fainted while walking down the street. As he fell, he had cut his face on the side of the curb. Maybe the only reason that the man was able to see his friend's ghost was because he had been reading at the time of the accident.

Tip 4: *Go to bed*

About one fourth of the people who see ghosts discover them immediately after they have woken up. Usually, they are awakened suddenly, just a few hours after they have fallen asleep. Consequently, the largest percentage of ghosts are seen when a person is in bed. Of course, if you've decided to look for a ghost who's been sighted along a highway, you're not going to take a sleeping bag and camp out there. This is sound advice only for those who are looking for ghosts in haunted houses.

According to ghosthunters Celia Green and Charles McCreery, one woman reported seeing a ghost after she had woken from a nap on a summer's day in New York City. She had just worked a sixteen-hour shift in a maternity ward and was due back at the hospital to work another shift in just a few hours. As she walked into her apartment building that sunny morning, she saw her building's superintendent, who told her that a plumbing inspector was coming to look at her apartment. Because she needed some sleep before returning to her job, she asked the super to postpone the plumber's visit as long as possible.

In her apartment, the woman took a shower and crawled into bed, totally exhausted. In moments, she was asleep. When she woke sometime later, she was aware that someone was in the room. She looked up and saw a man. She thought it was the plumber, and pulled the sheets over her head, furious that he had disturbed her sleep. Then she remembered that she had chain-locked her apartment door. Even if the super had un-locked the other locks, he could not have undone the chain.

At that moment, she raised her head from under the covers and tried to open her eyes, but they were glued shut. She couldn't move her body at all. Then the feel-ing passed. She opened her eyes and saw no one. When she checked the front door, the chain was in place.

Later, she tried to remember the man's appearance: he had white hair and wore a tweed sports coat. She had no idea who he was, but she had no doubt that her experience was real.

Tip 5: *Move to a new residence*

Many people see ghosts just after they have moved to another house or apartment. Maybe because the new house is unfamiliar to them, they are more susceptible to seeing ghosts — or at least imagining them. All of the creaks and nighttime noises that houses make may scare people into believing that their house is haunted. This happened in Cambridge, England, when the Lawson family moved into Abbey House in October 1903.

From the beginning, the Lawsons had little rest from the haunting. In fact, their first night in the house, a ghostly disturbance occurred outside the maids' rooms.

Two maids shared one room, while the nursemaid and the two Lawson children slept in another room across the hall. Around midnight, they were all roused by a tremendous banging sound at the doors to their rooms. The banging seemed to start at the top of the doors and work its way down to the bottom. Terrified, the two maids thought that the door would be ripped from its hinges. Then, as the banging died down and as reason took over, they wondered if the nursemaid had needed something and had banged to get attention. Maybe, they thought, they were just acting skittish in their new quarters in this dreary old house.

Cautiously, they opened the door to their room and looked out. When they saw nothing, they hurried across the hall to the nursemaid's room. There they found the nursemaid trying to console the two children, who had woken and were howling with fear. When they discovered that none of them had caused the banging, the three women huddled together in the nursemaid's room for the rest of the night and vowed that they would not spend another night in Abbey House.

The next morning, however, Professor Lawson reassured them when he told them that the family's Newfoundland dog had been responsible for the commotion. The dog had been looking for the children and had banged against the doors when it tried to find them. Of course, the professor knew very well that the freshly painted doors displayed no nail marks from the dog.

83

Thanks to the professor's lie, though, the maids remained. Fortunately for him, the banging never occurred again.

From that night on, the professor and his wife were able to document many other instances of haunting that took place during the years that they resided at Abbey House. Mrs. Lawson kept notes of the haunting as it progressed, and both Professor and Mrs. Lawson gave interviews to scientists who studied ghosts.

Although Abbey House had a number of ghosts, the main one was The Nun, who appeared repeatedly between midnight and 4 A.M. Dressed in a long, dark robe, she seemed to be around thirty years old. The Lawsons observed her many times as she walked across the master bedroom from the door to the foot of the bed. After a few moments, The Nun would turn, walk to the window, and vanish there.

Even their daughter, Jane, saw The Nun. Jane told her mother one morning that something had come in her bedroom during the night and stared at her; she was certain that it was a bear (perhaps because of The Nun's dark robe). Her brother, John, told his mother, "I *used* to be afraid of it when I was little, but I'm not now, because I know it's just God walking about and looking after us, and He sometimes forgets to be quiet when . . . we're all asleep." They both appeared to be describing The Nun.

Tip 6: *Visit a relative or a friend*

Sometimes people see ghosts when they stay overnight at a friend's or relative's house. This way, you might see a ghost who haunts a friend's house or might possibly be visited by a ghost who has tracked you down.

A French woman from Marseilles, the youngest daughter in a large family, was visiting a friend in Paris in 1852 when she woke from a sound sleep and saw that her room was brightly lit, as if it were on fire. Since this was before the time of electric lights, the woman thought that she had forgotten to put out her candle and that it had started a fire. She jumped out of bed to see what had happened and saw, at the foot of her bed, a coffin resting on two chairs. In the coffin was her father. When she put out her hand to touch him, the room went dark without warning. She reached for her matchbox to light a candle, but the coffin had disappeared by the time the candle was lit. Then she looked at her watch and wrote down the time: 12:40.

The next morning, she told her friend about the strange sight. The following day, she received a letter from her family in Marseilles, saying that her father had died suddenly two nights earlier at 12:40. Right before he died, he told the family gathered at his bedside that he wanted to see his youngest daughter once more. Although he could not accomplish this alive, his ghost managed to carry out his dying wish.

Tip 7: *Need help with a problem*

Sometimes ghosts of the dead return to help a person who has a problem. Of course, some problems are out of the control of ghosts, but others seem just right for a ghostly visit.

A woman whose mother had died recently was terrified of thunderstorms. One afternoon, a thunderstorm began when the woman was upstairs tending to her baby. At the first crash of thunder, she grabbed her child and hurried downstairs. As she reached the bottom of the stairs, in a panic, she felt pressure on her shoulder, as if someone had touched it. Then she heard her dead mother's voice say very clearly, "Don't be afraid, nothing will harm you." The woman was so relieved by the voice that she was able to overcome her fear.

Tip 8: *Trust your instincts*

If you sense that someone or something is behind you or on the other side of a door, don't ignore that sensation. Trust your instincts and turn around or open the door; you may see your ghost that way. Many people who have seen ghosts have reported that they sensed that someone was behind them. If you don't check for ghosts, you may miss the one that's waiting behind you.

One man who trusted his instincts was Frank Graham of St. Louis, Missouri. A traveling salesman, he was in St. Joseph, Missouri, on business one day. It was noon, and Mr. Graham was in his hotel room writing up orders and smoking a cigar. Suddenly, he became conscious of a presence. Rather than ignore the sensation, he turned and clearly saw his sister, who had died the year before. She was close enough to touch, and she looked perfectly alive. The only odd part of her appearance was a small scratch on her cheek. Excited to see his sister, he jumped up and called her name, but her apparition vanished.

Mr. Graham was so agitated by his experience that he left St. Joseph immediately and returned to his parents' house in St. Louis. He recounted the episode, but when he mentioned the scratch on his sister's cheek, his mother rose, trembling, to her feet and nearly fainted.

"No one could have known about that scratch," she told him, since she had accidentally scratched his sister as she lay in her coffin. To cover all traces of it, she had applied makeup to her daughter's cheek. No one detected the scratch at the funeral.

"I know you've seen your sister," she said, hugging him. "You couldn't be making this up."

Had he not trusted his instincts, however, he would have never seen his sister's ghost.

Tip 9: *Think young*

Did you know that young people have a better chance of seeing ghosts than anyone else? That's because they aren't biased against the supernatural. When they see something strange, they accept it instead of trying to explain it away. In fact, some ghosts seek out young people, perhaps for this very reason.

The Grey Lady of Cleve Court, in England, was one such ghost. She was the wife of a cruel former owner of the house. Her husband kept her locked in a room for many years. Finally, she died, deprived of her greatest desire: to have had a son or daughter. Although the house had probably been haunted for a long time, no record of haunting exists before 1920, when Lord and Lady Carson moved into the house with their one-year-old son, Edward.

Edward's bedroom was in the oldest part of the house, which was built sometime in the 1400s. When he was old enough to talk, he told his mother that he did not like the strange lady that he had seen walking in the hallway near his room.

"What did she look like?" Lady Carson asked her son.

"I don't know," Edward replied. "I've only seen her walking away."

Lord Carson's niece, Patricia, spent some time at Cleve Court when she was four years old. Her bedroom was right down the hall from Edward's, and one morning

she began to talk about the Grey Lady.

"What lady is this?" Lady Carson asked her.

"The one who stands by my bed. There she is," Patricia said, pointing to a corner of her room. Lady Carson saw no one, but from that time the room was known as the Ghost Room. Even the family's dogs would not enter it.

Other children who stayed at Cleve Court reported similar experiences: they saw a Grey Lady that adults could not see. Only after she had lived in the house for twenty-nine years did Lady Carson herself see the Grey Lady. Being young, in this case, definitely made a difference.

Tip 10: *Don't think about ghosts*

Wherever you decide to look for a ghost, you need to take your mind off the subject, or your chances of seeing a ghost are small. Almost everyone who has ever seen a ghost has reported that it happened unexpectedly. Finding a ghost may be like waiting for water to boil on your stove. If you watch, it seems to take forever. However, water will eventually boil, but you may not be lucky enough to see a ghost. Almost no one has seen a ghost by deciding that one should appear.

One girl reported to some English ghosthunters that she didn't expect to see a ghost when she came home from school one November afternoon. She passed by her grandparents' bedroom and saw her grandfather talking to her grandmother, who had been very ill. Her grandmother, dressed in a nightgown and robe, was seated on a small couch, combing and brushing her hair. The girl walked into the room and said hello to them.

"I'm glad you're well enough to be out of bed," she told her grandmother.

They talked for a few minutes, then her grandmother said, "Barbara, it would be best if you don't tell anyone I was up and that you spoke with me."

The girl was in her own bedroom before she realized what was wrong. She dropped her school books, her heart started racing, she got goose pimples. What she remembered was this: her grandmother had died a month earlier. Yet her grandmother had seemed so real that she had forgotten about her death. Since then, her grandfather had often sat alone in his bedroom, talking to himself.

She was afraid to leave her room. She waited until her parents came home and she could hear them preparing dinner before she went downstairs. Even then, she did not mention the ghost to anyone for several months. Finally, she told her mother, who thought her experience must have been a dream.

But Barbara was certain the encounter was real. Unfortunately, she never talked about it to her grandfather. Only he would have been able to prove that she had seen a ghost.

As you can tell, following all these tips will not be easy, especially the last one. How can you find ghosts if you're not supposed to think about them? Remember that the key is to distract your mind from what's happening around you so that you can see the ghost that may be there. That's why reading and sleeping are two good suggestions.

You should also be aware that many people who see a ghost don't realize until afterward that they've seen one. So don't get discouraged. The person that you're watching at the very moment you're feeling discouraged may turn out to be the ghost you've been waiting for.

Finally, remember that many people have seen ghosts who did not "go by the rules." You could be one of those people, too. Just keep an open mind and a positive attitude.

7. Writing a Ghost Report

If you should meet a ghost, don't take time to pat yourself on the back. You have work to do, and you must do it quickly.

As soon as your encounter is over, you must write down everything that you remember — exactly as it happened — in a Ghost Report. Even if you wake up in the middle of the night, see a ghost, and then feel groggy, don't wait until morning, when you might think that the experience was a dream. Hop out of bed, turn on a light, and start writing. Later, if other people become interested in your experience, they will want to know if you wrote about your ghost immediately or if you waited a few hours. If you waited, they may not trust your memory.

Too many people who see a ghost wait too long to write a report about it. Then, years after they've seen their ghost, they try to write what they remember. Unfortunately, their memories aren't very good. You want to be more like an English boy who, along with his twin brother, saw a ghost one night. He wrote in his Ghost Report:

> There was not the usual bright moonlight, but a watery moon, sickly-looking and very cloudy. The two of us had been asleep when, without any apparent reason, we awoke together. My eyes turned towards the bedroom door, and slowly a figure in dark clothes seemed to pass through the door from outside. I was rather frightened. The figure — that of a man — passed round each bed, and then stood at the bottom and beckoned to us both.

The twin realized that the ghost was his dead father. His face and head looked solid, but the rest of his body did not seem real. The boys exclaimed, "Daddy, speak to us."

> [But] the figure . . . seemed to walk through the wall and vanish. I looked at my watch and it was three o'clock. After a further doze I awakened again, found paper and pencil, and put down the events of the previous hour or so at 3:45 A.M.

You should be able to do even better than the boy who saw this ghost. Instead of waiting forty-five minutes, it would be better to write your Ghost Report immediately. To help you out, here's a form you can use to make sure you've written down all of the necessary information. The rest of the chapter will explain what kind of information your report should include.

94

Ghost Report
Ghost Information

Date Seen:_____ Time Seen: _____ A.M./P.M.

Exact location: _____

_____

Duration of experience : _____

_____

Were other people present? Indicate how many
and who they were.

Describe the experience.

Ghost's age: _____   Ghost's sex: Male/Female

Ghost Report
Observer Information

Name: _____

Address: _____

Birthdate: _____

Education: _____

Present occupation: _____

Have you ever seen a ghost before? If so, give all pertinent details.

Health at time of experience (include any medication taken):

Observer's background information (including personal and family situation:

Observer's explanation:

I attest to the fact that all of the above statements are True.

signed: _____

Date and time: _____

As you write your report, forget everything that you've learned about ghosts. If you try to fit your ghost into the facts presented in this book, you may be omitting some important details. Remember: every ghost is different. You shouldn't prejudge your ghost and make it conform to one of the categories of ghosts mentioned earlier. Just write what happened.

Even things that seem unimportant should be included in your report. What may seem unimportant to you may actually be a very important piece of information. The best rule to follow is: write everything that happened, no matter how strange or trivial the event seemed.

Here are the directions for filling out a Ghost Report:

Your first job is to make sure you give specific information about the date, time, and location of your encounter. You should know what time you saw the ghost and how long the ghost appeared to you. If you know you're seeing a ghost, look at a clock as soon as it has disappeared. If you don't realize until later, try to figure out about what time you saw the apparition. A good description of the exact location is important; a sketch of the area or a floor plan would be valuable to another ghosthunter.

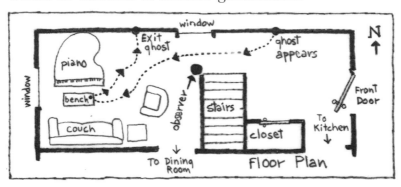

Mention whether other people were present, even if they did not see the ghost. If they did, have them fill out a report as well. Make sure you don't discuss the experience with them first; this will only cause others to disbelieve your story.

Describe what happened exactly as you remember it.

— Background information. What were you doing when you first saw the ghost? Could you have fallen asleep and dreamed the experience? If not, how do you know you were awake?

— First sighting. Did the ghost appear suddenly? Or did you awake to see it standing by you?

— Awareness of ghost. Exactly how could you tell that it was a ghost? Did it appear or disappear gradually? Did it have a strange expression on or color to its face? Was it the ghost of someone you know to be dead? What feelings did you have as you watched the ghost? Record all sensations that you remember: what did you see, hear, feel, or smell?

— Appearance of ghost. Was it white and filmy, of normal color, or a specific color or tint? Did it seem to be dark or shadowy or mostly bright? Did it appear to be three-dimensional or flat, as if it were a sheet of paper? Did it waver or seem transparent, or was it solid like a normal person? Describe its face thoroughly. Did it have dark or light hair? What color were its eyes? Try to indicate how tall the ghost was. Then describe the clothes it wore. What kind of clothes were they? Did they seem

98

old-fashioned or not? Were they stained anywhere? What type of fabric was the clothing made from, and what color was it? Mention any details that you can remember. If the ghost had any special features (a tattoo, unusual clothing or hair style, a certain look or attitude) or if the ghost was carrying an object, indicate this also.

— Emotional characteristics. Could you see or sense how the ghost was feeling? Was it laughing or happy? Was it angry? Did it cry? If so, did you actually see its tears? Or did it seem preoccupied or troubled? Whether you have real evidence of the ghost's feelings, describe all sensations that you have; make sure, though, that you make a distinction between what you actually saw and what your intuition told you.

— Activity. What did the ghost do during the time that you saw it? You might want to use the following list to indicate what your ghost was doing:

GHOST ACTIVITY

- [ ] standing still
- [ ] floating
- [ ] flying
- [ ] turning a corner
- [ ] walking
- [ ] sitting
- [ ] coming forward

- [ ] wandering aimlessly
- [ ] looking out window
- [ ] gliding
- [ ] lying down
- [ ] moving away
- [ ] moving in circles
- [ ] pacing
- [ ] dancing

— Personality. Describe your ghost's personality, which may seem hard to do. Again, trust your instincts. If the ghost seemed friendly, write that — even if you're not sure why you feel that way. Maybe later you'll be able to remember what made you think that the ghost was friendly. Here's a checklist of adjectives that could be used to describe a ghost. Try to indicate in your report which words describe your ghost:

GHOST PERSONALITY

☐ active	☐ fearful	☐ moody
☐ affectionate	☐ friendly	☐ noisy
☐ alert	☐ gentle	☐ patient
☐ anxious	☐ greedy	☐ quiet
☐ bitter	☐ helpful	☐ shy
☐ calm	☐ humorous	☐ strong
☐ changeable	☐ impatient	☐ tolerant
☐ cold	☐ independent	☐ trusting
☐ complaining	☐ irritable	☐ warm
☐ confused	☐ mischievous	☐ weak

— Communication between ghost and observer. Did the ghost look at you or did it ignore you? If it looked at you, did it act as though it recognized you? Was it afraid of you? Did the ghost talk to you? If it did, did you really hear the words, or were they communicated through ESP? What message did the ghost have for you?

— Conclusion. How did you lose sight of the ghost? Did it disappear or walk through a wall?

Finally, give your impression of the ghost's age and sex. It's important not to be afraid to use your intuition. If the ghost seemed old, guess at an age. Was it as old as your parents or grandparents? Or did it seem even older? Likewise, try to decide whether it was male or female. If the ghost was dressed in a long robe, it may be hard to tell unless you got a good look at its face. If you use your intuition, however, make sure you say so.

Once you've described your experience, you need to write a little about yourself. As you've seen in some of the stories in this book, some people could have made up a ghost story. A scientist would want to know some facts about you before deciding if your ghost was real or not.

First, you need to give some personal data. Make sure you include your birthday, how many years of schooling you've had, and (if you are finished with school) your present occupation.

Indicate whether you have had any other experiences with ghosts. This is useful information to a ghosthunter, especially if the person is a sensitive.

Describe your health at the time you saw the ghost. Were you feeling better or worse than normal? Were you coming down with a cold or just getting over the flu? Had you taken any aspirin or other medication before you saw the ghost? Any of these factors could affect your encounter.

Provide some relevant background information about you and your family. Were you upset about anything when you saw the ghost? If you had just received a bad grade in school or if your mother was ill or if a close friend had moved out of town, these factors should be included in your report, even if you weren't thinking about them at the time. Sometimes they may be important in understanding why the ghost appeared. Or, if you were staying with relatives or a friend when you saw the ghost, you should note that also.

Finally, in the last section of your report, you can write your own explanation of the ghost. What type of ghost do you think it was? Why do you think that it appeared to you? Why did the person become a ghost? No matter how silly some of your ideas may seem, put them down anyway. You probably know more than you think.

At the end of the report, you should put the time and date that you wrote it. Then you should sign the paper to certify that the experience really happened to you.

Once the report is done, it's important that you try to find someone else who also saw the ghost. If you were with a member of your family or a friend at the time you saw the ghost, you should ask that person to write a report — before you discuss your experience with him. If you talk about it before you both write it down, no one will ever know what you both *saw*, because you will be influenced by what the other person *said*. If you believe you saw the ghost of a person who might be living, you should show your report to someone and have him sign and date it. If you do meet that person in a few weeks (as Mr. Watson, the hotel owner, did), you will want to be able to prove that you saw the ghost long before the person actually died.

If you saw a ghost in your own house, you should ask other members of your family whether they have ever seen a ghost there. If someone says yes, ask him or her to write a report — before you tell what you saw. If that report matches yours, then you're beginning to prove that there's a ghost in residence. If the report doesn't match yours, either you have several ghosts in the house or you're imagining ghosts that don't really exist.

Finally, notify the American Society for Psychical Research, 5 West 73rd Street, New York, New York 10023. If your report sounds convincing enough and if the ghost is seen repeatedly, someone from the society may want to study the ghost you've seen. You can also send your report to Ghost-hunters (Box 398, Horseshoe Beach, Florida 32648), a newly formed organization for the serious study of ghosts.

After you've seen a ghost, though, you may find yourself wondering if you really saw it at all. Most people report that the experience of seeing a ghost seemed real enough at the time; afterward, though, they begin to have doubts. In that case, you want to prove that your ghost was real. The next chapter explains some ways to do that.

8. Becoming a Ghost Detective

If you're serious about proving that you or someone else saw a ghost, you must do some detective work afterward or people may think that you imagined the ghost.

"But I know what I saw," you might insist.

No one, especially a good ghosthunter, will believe your eyesight alone, no matter how convinced you are. People want evidence that a ghost is real, and getting evidence is not easy. Still, it can be done — if you see certain kinds of ghosts and if you have the right equipment.

In this chapter, you'll learn how to prove that three main kinds of ghosts exist: the ghost who is seen repeatedly, the ghost who is seen several times, and the poltergeist. The three other types of ghosts usually appear only once; to do any detective work on them, you'd need to see them again.

105

Investigation 1: *Detecting a ghost who is seen repeatedly or a ghost who is seen several times*

Imagine that your family has just moved into an old house. One night, you awaken to see a figure bending over your bed, but your room is so dark that you can't tell who it is. Then you become aware that you feel very cold. You close your eyes for a second. When you open them, you see nothing unusual, so you go back to sleep.

A few nights later, you awaken again. You're sure that you see the same figure bending over your bed. This time, you look at the figure more closely as it begins to move toward your open closet door. When it steps into your closet, a crack of light coming from your window illuminates the figure for a second. You see the back of a short man, dressed in a dark suit. Then the man vanishes into the closet. For a moment, you're sure that a burglar has broken into your house, but after waiting a few minutes and hearing nothing, you turn on your bedroom light and see that your closet is empty. The man you saw has disappeared.

Now you're confused. Did you see a ghost? Or were you imagining everything? Or could a strange person actually have been in your room?

To become a Ghost Detective and check this out, you will need some equipment:

GHOST DETECTIVE EQUIPMENT

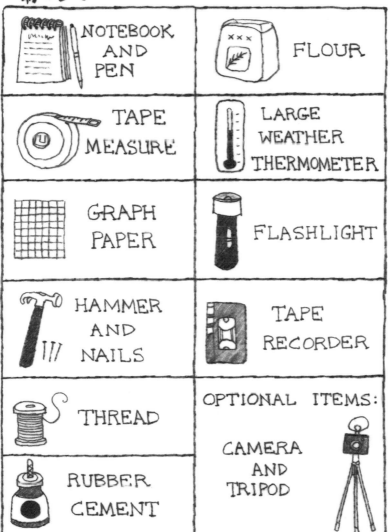

NOTEBOOK AND PEN	FLOUR
TAPE MEASURE	LARGE WEATHER THERMOMETER
GRAPH PAPER	FLASHLIGHT
HAMMER AND NAILS	TAPE RECORDER
THREAD	OPTIONAL ITEMS: CAMERA AND TRIPOD
RUBBER CEMENT	

At a minimum, you'll need a *notebook and pen* to take notes about the ghost. First, you must write your Ghost Report immediately. Then, the next morning, you must interview the members of your family to see whether they've had any strange experiences in the house. Has anyone heard eerie noises? Have any objects been misplaced or rearranged? Has anyone else seen anything unusual at night? If so, have them fill out a Ghost Report. Make sure, though, that you don't tell what you saw until you've interviewed everyone. If nothing was missing and there were no signs of a burglar, you might begin to believe that you really saw a ghost. But you still need proof. And if the ghost is the type who haunts a place regularly, you should be able to get the evidence you need if you continue your detective work.

A *tape measure* could also come in handy to note the distance between you and the ghost you saw. How far away was the ghost when you saw it? How far did it move across the room? This information should be included in your Ghost Report. Along with this, a piece of *graph paper* would be useful. You should draw a diagram of your bedroom as accurately as possible (use the tape measure to draw it to scale; usually, one square equals one foot), and indicate where the ghost was when you saw it first and where it moved before it disappeared. Perhaps this ghost (if it is a ghost) follows the same route every time it appears.

108

Then you'll need to search your room thoroughly. Start with your closet, since that's where the ghost seemed to disappear. The first question you must ask yourself is: could there be another way out of the closet? Search your closet carefully. Pound on the walls to see if any area sounds hollow. Check the floorboards to see if they are firmly in place. Are any parts of the wall boarded over? Is there a trap door to the attic in the ceiling of your closet?

Even if you find a secret room or an entrance to the attic, you may have seen a real ghost, not a burglar. The next thing you must do is get ready for the ghost in the event that it appears again.

First, you want to make sure that only a ghost could disappear in your closet. If there's an entrance to the attic, hammer some *small nails or thumbtacks* partway into the frame surrounding the attic opening. Space them a few inches apart.

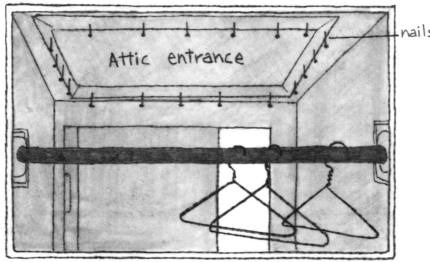

Once you've done that, take some *thread* and lace it around the nails and across the opening, so that you make a complex zigzag pattern that no one could pass through to get to the attic. This way, if you see the figure again, you can tell if you've caught a person. On the other hand, a ghost will be able to pass through the thread quite easily.

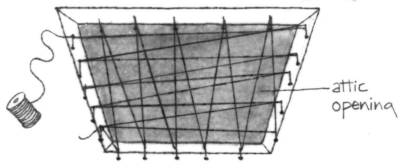

attic opening

Even if there is no other exit to your closet, you can take a piece of thread that's as wide as your closet door and, running it between the frame a few inches off the floor, attach it to both sides with some balls of *rubber cement*. If the ghost reappears and follows the same path to your closet, you can check to see what happened to the thread. A real ghost will not break the thread.

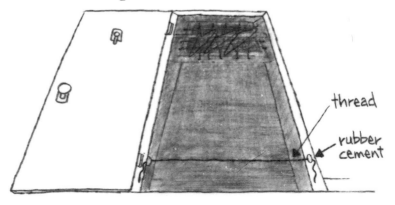

thread

rubber cement

Second, you can check to see whether your ghost is real by sprinkling *flour* between your bed and your closet. Only a real ghost will not leave footprints behind; if you see footprints, you probably didn't see a ghost.

Now you're ready to start your ghost stake-out, which means that you must stay up at least part of the night to see if the ghost reappears. You will need to set up a base of operations, such as a chair in the corner of your bedroom with a small table for the rest of your equipment.

During the night, probably at ten- or fifteen-minute intervals, you will want to check the temperature of your bedroom with a *thermometer*, preferably one that has a large face that can be easily read. Then you need to record the temperature on a piece of graph paper. When you felt chilled the night that you saw the ghost, did the room actually become colder? Or were you just frightened and shivery? The presence of a ghost may lower the room's temperature dramatically. If you keep the thermometer beside you, you will be able to check regularly.

Since you must try to capture the same conditions as the night you first saw the ghost, you should sit in the dark. For that reason, a *flashlight* is a necessity for reading both your watch and the thermometer.

Finally, if you can borrow a *flash camera with a tripod*, set it up beside you, facing the area where you first saw the ghost. If the ghost appears, you can try to take its picture. Keep in mind that this is one of the hardest things to do. Ghosts aren't known for photographing well.

Investigation 2: *Detecting a poltergeist*

Proving that a poltergeist exists is more frightening, especially if the poltergeist is real and likes to throw objects.

Imagine the following events. Your neighbor mentions to you that something scary is happening in his house. He was sitting on the couch in his living room last night when he saw the cushion next to him sink, as if someone invisible had sat next to him. Then, out of the corner of his eye, he saw an easy chair move a few inches to the right. Recently, he has heard a number of strange noises in the living room: knocking sounds, clicks, and tappings. At first, he thought his television was acting up, because he only heard the sounds when the television was on. But then he began to hear the sounds when the TV was off. Last night he was sure that a vase on the coffee table moved a few inches.

Could his house be haunted by a poltergeist? If you do good ghost detective work, you'll find out. But first, a warning. Never look for a poltergeist alone. It's always a good idea to take a friend to help you, even to a neighbor's house. You never know what you'll find, and another person could come in handy.

You'll need the following equipment to check for a poltergeist:

NOTEBOOK AND PAPER	FELT-TIP PEN
TAPE RECORDER	INDEX CARDS
MASKING TAPE	TYPING PAPER

By now, you should know the first step: interview your neighbor thoroughly. You may want to take notes, but most people can't write as fast as someone talks. Therefore, you should ask your neighbor whether you can use your *tape recorder* as you interview him. Try not to make him feel self-conscious with the microphone, and promise him that you will keep all information confidential, unless he gives you permission to share it with someone. Remember that no matter how much you want to find a ghost, you have to respect the privacy of anyone involved.

Some of the questions you will want to ask during your interview are:

When did the events first begin to happen? When was the last time that something happened? If the events were caused by a poltergeist, remember that poltergeist experiences don't last very long. Usually, a poltergeist will not continue to disturb people beyond a few months at most.

Exactly what has happened? Ask your neighbor to give you the dates and the times for each event, if he can. Have there been loud noises? Has anyone seen objects begin to move?

Who else lives in the house? What are their ages? A teenager is often thought to be the "haunted person."

Who was home when the events happened? If five people live in the house, but only one of them was home when all of the events happened, you might suspect that that one is the haunted person.

Is anyone new living in the house? Sometimes a newcomer may cause a poltergeist experience.

Can you think of any normal explanation for the experiences? For example, if a floor has a slight slant, something could easily roll off a table by itself.

Have others seen the strange events? Are they willing to be interviewed? The more witnesses there are, the more believable the poltergeist is.

Are only certain rooms in the house involved in the events? If the only room affected is the bedroom of a teenage son, you should suspect that the poltergeist is somehow connected to him. Try to interview the son, if possible.

Has anyone seen a ghost? If someone has, you may want to check for a ghost of the dead rather than a poltergeist.

When you're done interviewing your neighbor, you want to make sure that you write a Ghost Report for him. Include in your report some information about your neighbor, such as his age. But you will also want to write down some other things:

Does your neighbor wear glasses? If he does, are they bifocals? Perhaps he imagined the movement because of his glasses.

Is your neighbor colorblind? If he is, he might not be able to describe accurately what he saw.

Is your neighbor in good health? Was he taking any medicine? Some medicines might have caused him to imagine the movement.

After your interview, if you think there may be a poltergeist, you need to ask your neighbor's permission to do some experiments in his house, especially in his living room, if that is the only room that the poltergeist disturbs.

Once you have his permission, you should examine the house thoroughly, looking for anything suspicious. In this particular case, you would want to check the basement (if there is one) beneath the living room, the living room itself, and the rooms around it and above it. You should look for anything that could have caused the noises. Are there any animals in the house? Could a squirrel or a rat have gotten in between the walls? Are there any secret rooms?

As you move from room to room, tape all of the doors closed with *masking tape*. Don't tape the whole door frame; just put one large piece across the closed door and its frame. Then, using a *felt-tip pen*, write your name or make some other identifying mark, so that the tape cannot be replaced by anyone else. Do the same for all of the windows in the house; put the tape on the window and its frame, then use your pen. You want to make sure that no one else can get into or out of the house, and that no one can go into any rooms in the house — except the poltergeist.

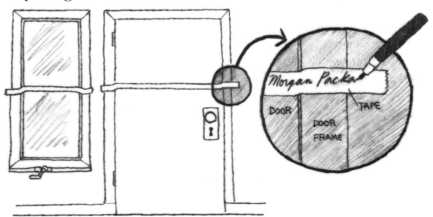

In the haunted room, make a careful examination. Are there cracks in the living room walls? If so, the house may be settling, which may have caused the unexplained noises; it may even have caused the chair to move. Are there any boarded-up doors between the living room and other rooms? You want to make sure that there are no hidden entrances into the room. Check the floorboards also. Are any of them loose and creaky?

Under the legs of the chair that was moved, tape *index cards* or *typing paper* to the floor. Then, trace the outline of each leg on the paper. If a poltergeist moves the chair, the legs will no longer be inside the outline on the paper. Do the same for any objects in a bookcase or a wall unit.

After you've finished all of your preparations, ask the members of the family to stay in one room, and seal them in with your masking tape. If you know that one member of the family is the haunted person, ask him or her to join you and your friend in the haunted room.

When all of you are stationed there, be patient and wait. Even though you're waiting for a poltergeist, try to act as normally as possible. Watch television or read a book, but don't keep staring at the clock. If the poltergeist feels like making its presence known, it will.

An important thing to watch for is how close the haunted person is to any object that is seen moving. As you watch an object in the room move, ask yourself: could the haunted person have moved the object himself? Sometimes people pretend to be haunted by poltergeists and invent clever ways to make things move. Remain alert and be suspicious. The closer the haunted person is to any moving object, the more suspicious you should be.

If you become a Ghost Detective and follow these suggestions, you should have no trouble proving that a ghost or poltergeist is real or not. You can adapt these ideas to any situation and almost any ghost by using creative thinking. If a ghost has been seen walking up and down a staircase, sprinkle the steps with flour and attach thread with rubber cement, a few inches off the step, from the banister to the wall. A ghost will not disturb the thread or leave footprints.

One Ghost Detective, from Springvale, Maine, wrote the American Society for Psychical Research in 1890 about his experiences investigating ghostly activity. One night, T. J. McDaniel was disturbed by the mysterious
118

rattling of his bedroom window. Since he suspected a ghost, he took some thin pieces of wood and wedged them between the window frame and its sash. No matter how hard he tried, he could not rattle the window.

After he returned to bed, though, the window began to shake again. Only then did he realize that the sound was not so much a rattle as it was a soft tapping. He looked out the window but saw nothing that could explain the noise. He had to listen to the tapping for an hour before it finally stopped. The next morning, he learned that his father had died during the night. Although Mr. McDaniel did not have proof that his father's ghost had tapped on his window, he had proved that the window was not rattling on its own.

One final warning: be careful not to make too many elaborate preparations for your ghost. The more a house is disturbed from its normal state, the less likely it is that a ghost will appear. And if you should decide to report your ghost to the news media, remember that when reporters or television crews show up to interview or film a ghost, it almost never appears.

What's more, no matter how hard you try, you may not be able to prove that the ghost you saw was real. The ghost may not appear again. Or it may appear but somehow manage to avoid your detective experiments. If that happens to you, you can look forward to seeing your next ghost and trying again.

9. Two More Ghost Stories

Now that you know how to hunt for ghosts and prove that they are real, here are two more stories to encourage you. Both are true, but they have very different outcomes.

Mr. and Mrs. Berini and their two children moved into their New England home in May 1979. Almost immediately, the Berinis heard a voice during the night.

"Mama, Mama, this is Serena," a girl's voice cried.

The Berinis knew of no one named Serena, but when they asked Mr. Berini's father, he recalled that his sister Serena had died in the same house at the age of five. Altogether, they heard Serena crying six times over the course of six months. After three of those occasions, the Berini family experienced either a catastrophic illness or death. For example, Serena cried for her mother the night before Daisy, the Berinis' daughter, suffered cardiac arrest while undergoing a tonsillectomy.

Serena's ghostly crying gave way to the figure of another ghost. On March 19, 1981, Mrs. Berini awoke to see the ghost of an eight- or nine-year-old boy dressed in white clothing: shirt, pants, and shoes.

"It was almost like looking through a milk bottle," Mrs. Berini told researchers later. "The boy would walk back and forth in the hallway. It was a very peaceful experience and I was not afraid. It stayed for about two hours on and off, coming and going."

The next night, the ghost reappeared, but this time it spoke to Mrs. Berini.

"Where do all the lonely people go?" it asked. "Where do I belong?"

When she told her husband, Mr. Berini believed the ghost was that of Giorgio, one of his father's brothers, who had died at eight. He had been buried in his white communion suit. A few days later, Mr. Berini himself saw Giorgio's ghost trying to pick up a rug in the upstairs hallway. When the ghost disappeared, Mr. Berini moved the rug and found a medallion of the Virgin Mary between the floorboards.

Over the course of the next two months, Giorgio appeared two or three times a week, sometimes to Mrs. Berini and sometimes to her husband. Many times he spoke to them. Once, he told Mr. Berini, "My oldest brother is the only one who can help me." Another time, he spoke of Carlos Berini, his twin brother, who still lived in another part of town. Giorgio's ghost accused Carlos of taking something from the Berinis' house.

When Mrs. Berini mentioned the ghost to her priest in

the middle of May, he suggested that the Berinis ignore it. During Giorgio's next appearance, on May 27, Mrs. Berini completely ignored his presence. In response, Giorgio slammed a closet door twenty times. A few days later, when the Berinis again ignored Giorgio, something pulled a package of macaroni from Mrs. Berini's hand, spilling its contents on the floor. On June 3, two other priests blessed the house with holy oils, but Giorgio's ghost returned the next night. Finally, Mr. Berini, following the instructions of another priest, commanded the ghost to leave in the name of Christ.

Giorgio's visits ended, but another ghost appeared, first on June 5 and again a few nights later. This figure wore a black cape and had a hump on its back. After its appearance, the receiver on the bedroom telephone kept flying across the room. Dishes and religious figurines were broken. A bookcase at the top of the stairs was twice found downstairs, and Daisy's desk once moved out of her room and down the stairs. The scene of the most violent activity was the upstairs hallway, where the retractable attic stairs opened and shut repeatedly, which caused the hall ceiling to crack. The family experienced no relief from these incidents until Daisy's birthday, August 28, when a carving knife was discovered stuck in the kitchen table. That night, the Berinis moved out of the house until a priest could perform an exorcism. When they moved back in on September 25, they experienced no further episodes.

This haunting is unusual for a number of reasons. First, three different ghosts appeared to the Berinis. Serena's and Giorgio's ghosts were seen repeatedly, while the caped ghost was seen only twice. Second, the ghosts became increasingly more troublesome. The Berinis heard Serena's voice for only six months, before Giorgio showed up. Giorgio was fairly temperamental, especially when he was ignored. But the caped ghost was positively scary, and its appearance was followed by significant poltergeist activity.

The most troubling aspect of this case, however, is that the Berinis did nothing to try to understand why the ghosts appeared. They listened to Serena cry for her mother, but not once did they ask Mr. Berini's grandmother (Serena's mother) about Serena or any specific details related to her death. Why did Serena want to see her mother so much? She had a wish that wanted to be fulfilled.

When Giorgio appeared, he, too, wanted to communicate with the Berinis, as Mr. Berini's discovery of the medallion of the Virgin Mary indicated. What did the medallion mean? Why was Giorgio's ghost so persistent? And what object was Carlos accused of taking? Rather than explore the possibilities, the Berinis ignored Giorgio, who had a major temper tantrum. If only Giorgio hadn't been ignored, perhaps the third ghost and the poltergeist activity that followed would never have happened.

124

The Berinis also missed the opportunity to prove that their ghosts were real. By the time ghosthunters were called in, the hauntings had stopped. What could the Berinis have done? First, they could have attempted to tape-record Serena's voice. Perhaps someone would have been able to identify the voice as Serena's. Second, they could have asked Carlos, Giorgio's twin brother, to help them understand why Giorgio was so upset. What could Carlos have taken? Why was Giorgio so troubled? Giorgio might have appeared to Carlos as well, which would have provided even more proof that Giorgio was real. Even Mr. Berini's grandparents could have been asked to help, since the ghost of their dead son was involved. Third, the Berinis could have contacted former residents of their house to see whether they had been troubled by any of the ghosts as well.

Although the Berinis did stop the haunting eventually, they missed an opportunity to understand why it happened in the first place. They needed to take a lesson from the next case and develop into Ghost Detectives.

About a hundred years before the Berinis' house was haunted, an eighteen-year-old girl named Rose Despard became a Ghost Detective when she discovered that her house in Cheltenham, England, was haunted. From her first meeting with a ghost, Rose decided to prove that it was real, a process that took over two years.

The Despard family moved into an ordinary, twenty-year-old house in April 1882, long before electric lights were invented. Two months later, Rose, the second-oldest daughter, was in her room one night preparing for bed when she heard someone pushing against her door. She thought it might be her mother, who was an invalid and not very strong. When she opened the door, no one was there. Carrying a candle for light, Rose stepped into the hallway and looked toward the stairway. At the top of the stairs, shrouded in darkness, she saw a tall lady dressed in black. In a moment, the strange woman began to walk down the stairs. Rose tried to follow her, but her candle had burned too low and went out. She returned to her room, sure that she had seen a ghost. That night, Rose decided to become a Ghost Detective and not talk about the ghost to her family until she was sure that it was real.

The next time she saw the ghost, Rose followed her downstairs to the living room. The woman in black stood to the right of a large window, then left the room and walked toward the back door of the house, where she disappeared.

At first, Rose thought that she was the only person who had seen the ghost. Then she discovered that three other people in the house had seen the woman in black around the same time, though they did not realize that she was a ghost. Rose's older sister, who was married and visiting the family for a few days, saw the woman in black one evening before dinner. As she sat down at the dining room table, she wondered aloud who the nun was that she had seen walking into the living room. Since there were many visitors to the large house, no one was suspicious that the nun might have been a ghost — except Rose, who was sure that the nun was the same woman in black she had seen.

During the next two years, Rose wrote letters about the ghost to a close friend of hers, so that she managed to write a Ghost Report of sorts. During this time, she also began to prove that her ghost was real.

She fastened some thread across the stairs after everyone had gone to bed. She put pellets of glue on the ends of each thread and fastened one end to the wall and the other to the banister. Two different times, she saw the woman in black pass through the thread without disturbing it.

She also reported how the family dogs acted when the woman in black was around. One dog, a terrier, ran along the upstairs hallway, its tail wagging, as if to greet someone. It jumped up in the air, expecting to be patted, then suddenly scooted away to hide with its tail between its legs. Rose realized that the dog must have seen the ghost, although she did not see the ghost at the same time.

Another experiment that Rose carried out was her attempt to touch the ghost. This was impossible, for every time Rose tried to get close enough to touch the woman, she seemed to be just beyond Rose's reach. When Rose tried to trap her in a corner of a room, the woman in black simply disappeared.

By the end of the two years, Rose had seen the ghost six times and had learned that some of her sisters had seen the ghost, too. In fact, her sisters had heard the woman in black's footsteps so often that they were afraid to open their bedroom doors at night if they heard someone walking by.

For some reason, during the summer of 1884, the woman in black appeared almost daily and so scared Rose's sisters and the servants that Rose decided to tell her father about the ghost. Mr. Despard had no idea that a ghost was in residence and was surprised that Rose had waited two years to tell him. The next day, a neighbor who lived across the street stopped by to say that he had seen a tall lady in a black dress crying in the Despards' backyard. She was wearing a bonnet and a veil covered her face; the neighbor thought that one of the family was in mourning. Mr. Despard realized that the description matched Rose's ghost.

Who was the lady in black? Was she in mourning? Why did she haunt the house so regularly?

It wasn't long before Rose and Mr. Despard began to check the history of the house. Here is what they found. A Mr. Swinhoe built the house in 1860 — and he lived there for seventeen years. Sometime during his residence, his wife died. He took it badly and began to drink heavily. Two years after her death, he married again. His new wife, Imogen, tried to stop his drinking, and when she failed, began to drink herself. They fought frequently and their lives together were miserable. Early in 1876, Imogen left him. Shortly afterward, he died in the house. Two years later, Imogen also died, and her body was brought back to the town to be buried.

Rose continued her detective work. She was certain that Imogen Swinhoe was the woman in black, a sign that the ghost was a widow. Who else had a reason to be dressed in widow's clothes besides Imogen? To get more proof, she interviewed Imogen's stepdaughter, who told Rose that her stepmother's favorite room in the house had been the living room, the same room in which Rose had observed the ghost so often.

She also learned something else of interest: Mr. Swinhoe died in the month of July, his first wife died in

August, and Imogen died in September. The woman in black was seen most often during those months, which might be explained by the dates of their death.

The most puzzling thing about the woman in black is that some members of the Despard family were never able to see her. One night, four years after the ghost had first appeared, Edith, one of Rose's sisters, was the last person to go upstairs. As she walked down the hallway to her room, two of her sisters called to her and said that they had heard some odd noises a few moments before. They had opened their doors and peered into the hall, and they saw the flame of a candle go down the hall as if carried by someone. But the person and the candle itself were not visible — only the burning flame. As the three sisters stood in the hall, holding their lighted candles, they heard footsteps approach them and then walk between them. As the footsteps passed, they felt a cold wind, but their candles were not blown out. The footsteps continued down the hall to the stairway.

After that experience, Rose had few other encounters with the woman in black. She wrote in a final Ghost Report, published by the British Society for Psychical Research, that by 1892 the woman hadn't been seen in three years, though her footsteps were still heard sometimes. By her dedicated research, Rose Despard provided good evidence that the ghost of Mrs. Swinhoe really existed — and, in fact, still exists. A number of sightings over the past twenty years suggest that Mrs. Swinhoe's ghost still haunts Rose's old house.

One more thing. Rose's research not only proved the existence of Mrs. Swinhoe but it prepared her for her future career. In 1895, Rose completed medical school, graduating with high honors. Not only was she among the first women doctors in England, she was definitely well prepared for the research, problem solving, and dedication that her profession demanded. Unlike the Berinis, Rose wanted to understand ghosts better.

As a ghosthunter and as a Ghost Detective, you should strive to do the same.

Acknowledgments

I would like to thank the American Society for Psychical Research for permitting me to use its extensive library. I am especially grateful to James G. Matlock, the society's librarian and archivist, for his assistance during my research, and to Karlis Osis, who unknowingly gave me the idea for this book.

I have relied on many sources in writing this book, including many issues of the journals published by the American and the British Society for Psychical Research. The following list presents a selected bibliography of material that was most useful to me:

Bennett, Sir Ernest. *Apparitions and Haunted Houses*. London: Faber and Faber, 1939.

Betty, L. Stafford. "The Kern City Poltergeist: A Case Severely Straining the Living Agent Hypothesis." *Journal of the Society for Psychical Research*, vol. 52 (October 1984), pp. 345–64.

———. "A Resentful Spirit (Part 2)." *Fate*, vol. 40 (October 1987), pp. 93–98.

Cortesi, Lawrence. "Albany's Capitol Ghost." *Fate*, vol. 38 (February 1985), pp. 67–73.

Ebon, Martin (ed.). *True Experiences with Ghosts*. New York: New American Library, 1968.

Gauld, Alan, and A. D. Cornell. *Poltergeists*. London: Routledge and Kegan Paul, 1979.

Green, Andrew. *Ghost Hunting: A Practical Guide*. London: Garnstone Press, 1973.

———. *Ghosts of Today*. London: Kaye and Ward, 1980.

Green, Celia, and Charles McCreery. *Apparitions*. London: Hamish Hamilton, 1975.

"How to Measure a Ghost (Part 1)." *Ghost-Hunter's Report*, vol. 7 (June 1987), pp. 2–4.

MacKenzie, Andrew. *Hauntings and Apparitions*. London: Granada, 1983.

———. *The Seen and the Unseen*. London: Weidenfeld and Nicolson, 1987.

Maher, Michaeleen, and Gertrude R. Schmeidler. "Quantitative Investigation of a Recurrent Apparition." *Journal of the American Society for Psychical Research*, vol. 69 (October 1975), pp. 341–51.

Matthews, Fred M., and Gerald F. Solfvin. "A Case of RSPK in Massachusetts: Part I — Poltergeist. Part II — The Haunting." In J. D. Morris, W. G. Roll, and R. L. Morris (eds.), *Research in Parapsychology 1976*. Metuchen, N.J.: Scarecrow Press, 1977.

Moss, Thelma, and Gertrude R. Schmeidler. "Quantitative Investigation of a 'Haunted House' with Sensitives and a Control Group." *Journal of the American Society for Psychical Research*, vol. 62 (October 1968), pp. 399–410.

Nisbet, Brian C. "The Investigation of Spontaneous Cases: Some Practical Suggestions." In Ivor Grattan-Guinness (ed.), *Psychical Research*. Wellingborough, England: Aquarian Press, 1982.

Osis, Karlis. "Characteristics of Purposeful Action in an Apparition Case." *Journal of the American Society for Psychical Research*, vol. 80 (April 1986), pp. 175–93.

Owen, A. R. G. *Can We Explain the Poltergeist?* New York: Garrett Publications, 1964.

Rhine, Louisa E. "Hallucinatory Psi Experiences II: The Initiative of the Percipient in Hallucinations of the Living, the Dying, and the Dead." *Journal of Parapsychology*, vol. 21 (March 1957), pp. 13–46.

Rogo, D. Scott. *An Experience of Phantoms.* New York: Taplinger Publishing, 1974.

Roll, William G. *The Poltergeist.* London: Wyndham Publications, 1972.

Roll, William G., and Steven Tringale. "A Haunting-Type RSPK Case in New England." In W. G. Roll, J. Beloff, and R. A. White (eds.), *Research in Parapsychology 1982.* Metuchen, N.J.: Scarecrow Press, 1983.

Schmeidler, Gertrude R. "Quantitative Investigation of a 'Haunted House.' " *Journal of the American Society for Psychical Research*, vol. 60 (April 1966), pp. 137–49.

Smith, Susy. *Ghosts Around the House.* New York: World Publishing, 1970.

Underwood, Peter. *A Gazetteer of British Ghosts.* London: Pan Books, 1971.

For Further Reading

Anderson, Jean. *The Haunting of America*. Boston, Mass.: Houghton Mifflin, 1973.

Aylesworth, Thomas G. *Vampires and Other Ghosts*. Reading, Mass.: Addison-Wesley, 1973.

Cohen, Daniel. *America's Very Own Ghosts*. New York: Dodd, Mead, 1985.

———. *Ghostly Terrors*. New York: Dodd, Mead, 1981.

———. *The Restless Dead: Ghostly Tales from Around the World*. New York: Dodd, Mead, 1984.

Harter, Walter L. *Osceola's Head and Other American Ghost Stories*. Englewood Cliffs, N.J.: Prentice-Hall, 1974.

———. *The Phantom Hand and Other American Hauntings*. Englewood Cliffs, N.J.: Prentice-Hall, 1976.

Knight, David. *The Haunted Souvenir Warehouse*. Garden City, N.Y.: Doubleday, 1978.

———. *The Moving Coffins: Ghosts and Hauntings Around the World*. Englewood Cliffs, N.J.: Prentice-Hall, 1983.

Index